Zebulon B. Vance
and
"The Scattered Nation"

Zebulon B. Vance
and
"The Scattered Nation"

Zebulon B. Vance
and
"The Scattered Nation"

MAURICE A. WEINSTEIN

Editor

The Wildacres Press
Charlotte, N. C.
1995

Published May, 1995

Published by
The Wildacres Press
Charlotte, N. C.

Library of Congress Catalog Card Number: 95–60697
International Standard Book Number:
ISBN 0–9646363–0–1

Design by Jim Billingsley
Printed Letterpress in the United States of America
by Heritage Printers, Inc.
Charlotte, N. C.

Dedicated to the memory of
I. D. BLUMENTHAL
*philanthropist, creator of humanitarian institutions
and devotee of Zebulon B. Vance.*

Acknowledgments

Although I have been interested in the life and accomplishments of Zebulon B. Vance for many years, it was at the suggestion of Herman Blumenthal, chairman of the Blumenthal Foundation, that I decided to perform the research and preparation of this work. I am grateful for his encouragement from the inception and along the way to completion.

I thank John B. Boles, Managing Editor of the Journal of Southern History for permission to republish "Zebulon B. Vance and the Scattered Nation" by Selig Adler. (The Journal of Southern History, Vol. VII, August 1941. No. 3.)

A debt of gratitude is due Dr. Irving J. Edelman for his assistance in preparation of the bibliography.

A special measure of gratitude is extended to my longtime secretary, Joan O. Garner, for her diligent typing of the manuscript.

I am grateful to Mary Norton Kratt, eminent Charlotte historian, for her invaluable advice.

I am also thankful to Mildred H. Irvin for her reading the manuscript and her important suggestions.

I express appreciation to the staff of the North Carolina Division of Archives and History for their courteous assistance.

MAURICE A. WEINSTEIN
Editor

December 1994

Preface

"Of making many books there is no end" (Ecclesiastes 12:12). The proliferation of books has been a common practice for over two millennia. For a book to be meaningful, however, it should be of literary worth, satisfy a need and fill a void. I am convinced that this volume meets all these criteria.

Zebulon B. Vance is North Carolina's most renowned statesman, and 1994 is the 100th anniversary of his demise. It is regrettable that few people today recognize his name, let alone his achievements. It would, therefore, be most appropriate that his memory be honored at this time with a biographical sketch of his life, depicting his accomplishments and impact on North Carolina and the country.

A magnificent orator, Vance has been acclaimed for "The Scattered Nation," a speech he wrote that is regarded as the finest and greatest oration of his career. A masterpiece, it includes the contributions of the Jewish people and an impassioned plea that they be befriended. Last published in 1928, the speech is included in this volume so that it may be preserved for posterity.

Why did Vance, born in a log cabin in the North Carolina mountains, involved in many pursuits, prepare "The Scattered Nation" and deliver it throughout the United States over a period of 15 to 20 years? This phenomenon fascinated a Professor of History at the University of Buffalo, Selig Adler, who researched this perplexing question. His findings are presented in an article published in the

Journal of Southern History in August 1941 and is also included in this publication.

The memory of Vance would have faded wholly into oblivion were it not for Asheville, North Carolina, which had dedicated a towering monument in the center of the city to him and annually conducts a memorial ceremony on his birthday. A museum containing his memorabilia is located nearby.

In Charlotte, where he had practiced law for 10 years, the city had established a Vance Park and named a street and school for him. They, however, no longer exist.

The only memorials that do remain are a hard-to-find marker where his home stood, a bust of him at the Charlotte-Mecklenburg Library, and a small bronze plaque at the First Presbyterian Church on the pew where he and his family sat.

It is our fervent hope that by means of this book the memory of this distinguished statesman will remain alive and that he will take his rightful place in the annals of our country. Zebulon B. Vance deserves to be remembered, revered and commemorated.

HERMAN BLUMENTHAL
Chairman
The Blumenthal Foundation

Contents

APPENDICES

Illustrations

Chronology

1830	May 13, Born at Reems Creek Valley
1851	Attended University of North Carolina
1851	Admitted to bar at Asheville
1853	Married to Harriett Newall Espy
1854	Elected to North Carolina House of Commons
1858	Elected to United States House of Representatives
1859	Reelected to United States House of Representatives
1861	Colonel in Confederate Army
1862	Elected Governor of North Carolina
1864	Reelected Governor of North Carolina
1866—76	Practiced law in Charlotte
1868—73	Estimated time of first delivery of "The Scattered Nation"
1876	Reelected Governor of North Carolina
1878	Harriett Newall Espy Vance passed away
1879	Elected to United States Senate
1880	Married to Florence Steele Martin
1885	Reelected to United States Senate
1891	Reelected to United States Senate
1894	April 14, Zebulon B. Vance passed away

Zebulon B. Vance, a Renowned Statesman

CHAPTER ONE

Zebulon B. Vance, a Renowned Statesman

by Maurice A. Weinstein, *Editor*

*"Everything that men do or think
concerns the satisfaction of the needs they feel
or the escape from pain."*
ALBERT EINSTEIN

This is the story of Zebulon Baird Vance, who was born in a log cabin in the mountains of North Carolina and rose to become a renowned statesman.

He was twice elected to the United States House of Representatives, three times as Governor of North Carolina, and three times to the United States Senate.

The focus of this work is Zebulon B. Vance and his oration: "The Scattered Nation." However, to limit this book to that aspect alone would deprive the reader of the wide scope of the unique career of Vance and his relationship to "The Scattered Nation." Accordingly, this chapter will review the life of Vance, not only for that purpose, but also to revive the memory of the man and his outstanding achievements.

ELOQUENCE

Vance was a dynamic and powerful speaker; before juries and other audiences, he was a spellbinder. His speeches, both impromptu and prepared, were replete with humor, wit and wisdom. He possessed and used a bottomless well of anecdotes and jokes—not to entertain, but to illustrate his concepts and to make his points. He was a master of sarcasm, satire, and ridicule. Especially in campaigns in the mountains, he was known to tell off-color jokes.

Vance's impressive appearance enhanced his oratorical ability. In 1916, at the unveiling of the statue of Vance in Statuary Hall of the United States Capitol, the Governor of North Carolina, Locke Craig, remarked:

> His personal appearance was unique. He did not look like other men. No man who saw him ever forgot him. His magnetism charmed with a peculiar and indescribable power. When you looked upon him, you knew that you beheld the lion-hearted leader of men.[1]

Vance practiced law in Charlotte, North Carolina, for ten years, from 1866 to 1876. Charlotte was a small town; the 1860 census was 2,265, and in 1870, 4,473.

When Vance appeared in trials in the old courthouse on South Tryon Street in Charlotte, the stores on the Square closed; no need to be open, almost everyone was at the courthouse, or trying to get in, to hear Zeb Vance. Vance usually convinced juries of the righteousness of his causes. There was an important exception: In Statesville he defended Tom Dooley (Dula) in a murder case arising out of a love triangle; Vance served without fee because Dooley was destitute and a Civil War veteran. Dooley was found guilty and sentenced to be hanged. The trial sparked the famous ballad: "Hang down your head, Tom Dooley, hang down your head and cry."

Judge David Schenck, who presided over trials in which Vance appeared, wrote in his diary that Vance was:

> . . . an orator of unexampled power both in the power of his imagination and the force of his language; he handles pathos with delicate tenderness and wields the fierceness of satire with piercing sharpness. But as a humorist he has no equal, perhaps on the continent.[2]

In 1864, while War Governor, Vance went to Virginia on a speaking tour to visit the North Carolina troops of General Robert E. Lee's Army. Vance was honored with a review of the brigades; General Lee and Vance rode side by side. After the review, Vance addressed the troops. General J.E.B. Stuart, commander of the cavalry, after the speech said: "If the test of eloquence is its effect, this speech was the most eloquent ever delivered."[3] Dr. Edward Warren, who accompanied Vance, later wrote: "I heard General Lee remark that Governor Vance's visit to the army has been equivalent to its reinforcement by fifty thousand men."[4] No doubt, Vance delivered a stirring address; the troops were deeply moved and captivated. Obviously, Generals Stuart and Lee were carried away and engaged in hyperbole to express their enthusiasm.

Vance's manner of speech was florid and ornate in keeping with the style of 19th century oratory, as you will note in "The Scattered Nation." Vance's thoughts flowed freely: "To keep pace with his rapid flow of thoughts, Vance spoke with lightning-like speed."[5]

I have heard it said that the rules for a good speech are: "Be sincere, be brief and be seated." Vance was always sincere, but he frequently violated the other two admonitions.

There were times when he spoke for two and a half hours. Today, if a speaker exceeds an hour, he would gradually lose his audience, except for those who are asleep. Not so with Vance: He always held the attention of his audience throughout.

At the present time, high governmental officials retain speechwriters to prepare their speeches. Not Vance. He always prepared his lectures and without help from others —frequently by candlelight or oil lamp. Of course, his extemporaneous speeches needed no preparation and they were outstanding.

Vance's articulateness is well established. What about the substance, content and ideas expressed in his lectures? A fortuitous event often turns or determines the course of a person's life. In Vance's life, that event occurred on November 6, 1827, three years before he was born: a duel between Dr. Robert B. Vance of Asheville, an uncle of Zeb Vance, and Samuel P. Carson of Morganton, a Congressman.

In 1823, Carson had encouraged Dr. Vance to run for Congress against Felix Walker—who had been one of Daniel Boone's companions. Dr. Vance won by one vote. After one term Carson decided to run for Congress against Dr. Vance and defeated him. During the campaign the candidates hurled insults against each other causing intense antagonism. Carson challenged Dr. Vance to a duel and the offer was accepted. Duels were unlawful in North Carolina, so they held the event across the South Carolina line at Saluda Gap—a marker designates the place.

Among those present was Davy Crockett ("Davy, Davy Crockett, king of the wild frontier"), the coach who had been instructing Carson in the use of the pistol. On the signal, Carson fired and the bullet struck Dr. Vance. It was fatal.

Prior to the duel, Dr. Vance prepared his will in which he bequeathed his library of about five hundred volumes of classical literature to Zeb Vance's father, David Vance,

II. Among the books were the works of Tacitus, Cicero, Scott, Swift, Pope, Byron, Shakespeare, Milton and the Bible.[6] Zeb Vance's mother read to her children from the books, and, inspired by her, Zeb became a diligent reader. He remembered much of what he read, and that retention is revealed in his lectures as you will see in "The Scattered Nation." He was a student throughout his life. "He became a man who knew the use and power of words. Words were his tools; words sent him off to leadership and greatness. They made him an orator, and where could they have sprung from except these books?"[7]

Illustrative of his erudition is his commencement address at Wake Forest College in 1872, while he was practicing law in Charlotte:

> Nor can we rely upon the spread of learning and intelligence, to preserve the free institutions of our fathers in all their vigor and purity. History is a wonderful destroyer of theories, and this fond one of ours is likely to be overthrown by facts. If intelligence and virtue were synonymous, our confidence in it would be justified. But educated men are no more virtuous than ignorance is always wicked. And I believe that educated bad men, in all ages, have done more hurt to the world than all the ignorance that has ever existed. How many nations have lost their liberties through the wickedness of the learned? The brightest age of Athenian eloquence, philosophy and art, made the least resistance to corruption. The noblest orator, and the greatest poet of the Augustan age of Roman letters vied in the glorification of despotism and venality. The polite reign of Charles II rotted England to the core, and laid her liberties so low that only revolution and a change of dynasty could revive them. . . .[8]

In 1868, Vance delivered the eulogy at a memorial ceremony for David L. Swain, a dear friend of Vance, a former governor and long-time President of the University of North Carolina.

Vance was offered the presidency of the University of North Carolina, but respectfully declined.

Davidson College and the University of North Carolina awarded Vance honorary doctorate degrees.

HERITAGE

Zebulon B. Vance came from a long lineage of patriots and public servants. His grandfather, David Vance I, was a Lieutenant Colonel in the Revolutionary War; he fought in battles at Kings Mountain, Brandywine, Germantown and Valley Forge. David I was of Scotch-Irish descent. In 1775 he married Priscilla Brank, who lived in Burke County and was of German descent. After the war, Vance I acquired land along Reems Creek Valley near Asheville, and there he built a cabin of pine logs. David I and Priscilla had eight children—one wonders after seeing the restored log cabin, how they crammed eight children into that log cabin. One of the children was David II, who became the father of Zebulon B. Vance.

David II married Mira Margaret Baird in 1825. They also had eight children and lived in the same log cabin. Her father was Zebulon Baird—that's where Zebulon B. Vance obtained his first and middle names. Zebulon Vance was born in 1830, at the time Andrew Jackson was President of the United States. Zebulon Baird cleared the land that became Asheville. David II enlisted in the War of 1812, but before he was called to duty, the war was over.

Vance's brother, Robert B. Vance, was a Brigadier General in the Confederate Army. An uncle, Dr. Robert Brank Vance, was a member of the United States House of Representatives.

Frontis W. Johnston, Professor of History at Davidson College, summarized the heritage of Zebulon B. Vance:

> Above all there was received from both sides of the family a sense of public duty and a tradition of pub-

English influence?

lic service. His immediate ancestors had served thirteen terms in the North Carolina House of Commons and six terms in the North Carolina Senate. His two grandfathers had served for more than a score of years as the first clerks of court of their respective counties. In addition, his ancestors had enlisted in both wars in which his country had been involved at the time of his own birth; his uncle had been a United States Congressman; his brother was to serve eight years as clerk of court and six terms in the United States House of Representatives, as well as shorter terms in the State Legislature and in the United States Treasury Department. The career of Zebulon Baird Vance in both war and public office must have appeared to him but a fulfillment of family tradition.[9]

An integral part of Vance's heritage was the beauty of the mountains that surrounded Reems Creek Valley. In reading "The Scattered Nation," you will note descriptions of the mountains to illustrate points.

In 1850 he studied law under John W. Woodfin, an Asheville lawyer. Afterwards, he wrote to David L. Swain, President of the University of North Carolina, a former Governor and a former sweetheart of Vance's mother, to request a loan of $200 to help pay for one year at the University. The loan was granted, and he was admitted to the University. He arrived at Chapel Hill in July, 1851, where he engaged in general studies and law. Swain became a lifelong friend and advisor to Vance. Swain taught constitutional, international and moral law, and Vance was one of his students. The teachings of Swain influenced Vance throughout his career—especially in the area of individual freedom. Close friendships were also formed with Kemp P. Battle and his brother, Richard H. Battle, both of whom played important roles in Vance's career. In 1900 Richard H. Battle delivered the address at the unveiling of the statue of Vance on the capitol grounds in Raleigh.

In 1851 Vance was admitted to the bar, and entered the practice of law in Asheville. In 1852 he was elected solicitor

of Buncombe County; his opponent was Augustus Merriman—later to become Chief Justice of the Supreme Court
of North Carolina and United States Senator. Vance was
on his way to launching a career that would lead to his becoming a renowned statesman.

POLITICAL CAREER LAUNCHED

In 1854, Vance raised his political ambition beyond the
horizon of the mountains. Vance was a Whig because of
this party's pro-Union propensities, which coincided with
his firm beliefs. The Democratic Party tended to encourage
states' rights. He announced as a candidate for the House
of Commons—a holdover name from the House of Commons in England—the name was changed to the House of
Representatives in 1868. His opponent, Daniel Reynolds,
claimed that Vance was too young for the office he sought;
Vance was then 24. Vance retorted: "I must admit I am
young, but it is not my fault. My parents did not consult
me as to the time when I should be born. All I can do is to
promise to try to do better next time."[10] He should have
added: "That's something that time will remedy." He was
elected.

Next, Vance ran for the North Carolina Senate and was
defeated by David Coleman. In 1857 Vance was a candidate
for election to the United States House of Representatives
against the prominent Thomas Lanier Clingman, a long-
time member of the House of Representatives. Again,
Vance went down to defeat.

In 1858, Clingman was appointed to the United States
Senate. A special election was held to fill the vacancy.
Vance was undaunted, and at the age of twenty-eight an-
nounced that he would seek election to the United States
House of Representatives as a member of the American
Know-Nothing Party. His opponent was William W. Av-
ery for the Democratic Party, a prominent leader from

Burke County. There was an intense campaign over the fifteen counties, including Buncombe County, in the district. The campaign "set the mountains on fire."[11] At one stop, Vance arrived with a crowd of men leaping and dancing around him as he played the fiddle."[12] Vance condemned the secessionist proclivity of the Democrats and declared vehemently for the Union. Vance was victorious.

In December 1858, Vance went to Washington to enter the United States House of Representatives—a long way from the log cabin on Reems Creek. One of his colleagues wrote about Vance that he was "strong in integrity, wondrous in vitality . . . and a strict Federalist after an intense union pattern. His voice was never heard at Washington for disunion."[13]

He criticized the treasury deficit: "As we are in debt, and spending more than our income, and as our income is derived principally from the tariff, we have to do one of three things: either raise the income, lower our expenses, or walk into the insolvent court. . . ."[14] It sounds like the current days.

In 1859, Vance ran for reelection to the United States House of Representatives; this time in behalf of the Whig Party. His opponent was David Coleman for the Democratic Party, the man who defeated Vance when he ran for the North Carolina Senate. Vance defeated Coleman by a margin of seventeen hundred votes. The Congress convened on December 5, 1859.

The dark clouds of secession and war were on the horizon; there was a mounting controversy between the abolitionists of the North and the secessionists of the South.

In Congress and in North Carolina, Vance spoke out for union and against secession. In 1860, a Whig convention was held in Salisbury at which Vance delivered two stirring pro-Union addresses. Richard H. Battle wrote that he ". . . held up to their gaze a dark picture of the horrors to follow secession and disunion, all became subject to his magnetism . . . and when he closed, the streets of the town and the hills around long reverberated with their enthusiastic shouts."[15] Up to this time Vance was principally known in the mountains; now, his fame was growing across North Carolina. Among those present was William A. Graham, a former governor, senator and Secretary of the Navy; he became a long-time friend and advisor of Vance.

On November 30, 1860, two members of Congress from South Carolina, Boyce and Ashmore, addressed a crowd in Raleigh in which they favored secession. Afterwards, across the street Vance delivered a speech that lasted two hours. Boyce and Ashmore said that if the South seceded, it would have the protection of England. To this Vance responded that "it would be a protection that our forefathers had waged a seven years war to escape." His humble grandfather, Vance said, "had shed his blood to escape this protection, and now his grandson was called upon to fight to regain it."[16]

Abraham Lincoln was elected President on November 5, 1860, and inaugurated on March 4, 1861. Lincoln's election precipitated the secession of the states in the lower South; South Carolina left the Union on December 20, 1860. On April 13, 1861, Fort Sumter, at Charleston, was bombarded and surrendered to the Confederacy.

When Fort Sumter was fired upon and President Lincoln called upon North Carolina to furnish seventy-five thousand soldiers for the Union forces (declined by Governor John W. Ellis), Vance changed his mind. Here are his words:

> For myself, I will say that I was canvassing for the Union with all my strength; I was addressing a large and excited crowd, large numbers of whom were armed, and literally had my arm extended upward in pleading for peace and the Union of our Fathers, when the telegraphic news was announced of the firing on Sumter and [the] President's call for seventy-five thousand volunteers.

> When my hand came down from that impassioned gesti-
> culation, it fell slowly and sadly by the side of a Secession-
> ist. I immediately, with altered voice and manner, called
> upon the assembled multitude to volunteer, not to fight
> against but for South Carolina.[17]

Secession by North Carolina was becoming inevitable; on April 15, 1861, Governor Ellis ordered the occupation of Forts Macon, Caswell and Johnston—the coastal forti-fications.[18] "On April 20, a company of Charlotte Greys seized the mint, and ten days later, . . . the arsenal [at Fay-etteville] surrendered. . . ."[19]

On May 20, 1861, a convention created by the General Assembly of North Carolina voted for secession, and also ratified the Provisional Constitution of the Confederate States of America. North Carolina was the last State to join the Confederacy.

It was necessary for Vance to leave Congress because his State was no longer one of the states of the United States of America.

Vance organized a company of volunteers, and, as its Captain, marched to war. Later he was promoted to Colonel of the Twenty-Sixth North Carolina Regiment. He led his troops into battle at New Bern and Malvern Hill. "He became something of a hero throughout the State. . . ."[20]

THE WAR GOVERNOR

August 6, 1862, was the date to elect a new Governor of North Carolina. William W. Holden, editor of *The Weekly Standard* in Raleigh organized the Conservative Party—a new one. Holden proposed and supported Vance for Gov-ernor. Augustus S. Merriman visited the editor of *The Fayetteville Observer*, a prominent newspaper, and secured an endorsement for Vance. There was no party convention that selected a candidate; Vance was selected by consensus of many leaders and newspapers.

The other candidate was William Johnston of Charlotte, a railroad official, running under the banner of the Confederate party. The election was unique: There was no campaigning, no speeches, no platforms, no public gatherings, no paid advertisements and no managers. Vance relied upon his record, his fame, his diligence and his reputation for truthfulness. The campaigning was by newspapers supporting one candidate or the other. Vance remained in command of his regiment at Petersburg; he made an announcement that "a true man should . . . be willing to serve wherever the public voice may assign him. . . . I should consider it the crowning glory of my life to be placed in a position where I could most advance the interests and honor of North Carolina."[21]

Vance at the age of thirty-two was elected Governor of North Carolina by a landslide.

The band of the 26th Regiment came to the inauguration and played while the crowd gathered, including the "Governor Vance's Inauguration March" composed for the occasion. Vance, as usual, delivered a stirring address. He promised a vigorous prosecution of the war, and further declared "to hold the helm during . . . the great storm; to manage . . . public liabilities; to search out the talent and worth of the country and to bring it into the service of the State; and to clothe and organize our troops and to do justice to merit in the field."[22]

Celebrating an inauguration was one thing, but confronting tumultuous times, in the midst of a war, was another and a perplexing matter. The Union forces occupied Roanoke Island and New Bern and threatened further advances.

Soon after the inauguration, Lee's army suffered defeat and retreat at the battle of Sharpsburg-Antietam, with thousands of dead and wounded. Vance called upon Surgeon General Warren to collect surgical and medical supplies; then both were off to Virginia to help the returning

A. Vance's birthplace in Reems Creek Valley, Courtesy of N.C. Department of Transportation.

B. Zebulon B. Vance, age 28. Elected to U.S. House of Representatives. Courtesy of N.C. Division of Archives and History.

C. Vance's first law office in Asheville, 1851. From Dowd, Clement, *Life of Vance*, (Charlotte, 1897).

D. Three Confederate colonels: (L to R) J. R. Lane, H. K. Burgwin and Zebulon B. Vance in 1861. Painting by W. G. Randall. Courtesy N.C. Division of Archives and History.

E. Vance's desk located at Vance Museum in Reems Creek Valley. On this desk, "The Scattered Nation" was prepared at Charlotte. Photographer: Randall Cox.

F. Vance Monument at Pack Square in Asheville (1898). Photographer: Randall Cox.

G. Vance at age 36 when he arrived in Charlotte. From Dowd, Clement, *Life of Vance*, (Charlotte, 1897).

H. Vance's Charlotte residence, 1866–1876. From Dowd, Clement, *Life of Vance* (Charlotte, 1897).

I. Statue at Capitol Square, Raleigh (1900). Courtesy of N.C. Division of Archives and History.

J. Statue of Vance in Statuary Hall in the Capitol, Washington (unveiled 1916).

It appears that L Vance was the best
provider for families of soldiers of any
of confederate governors ~
· RENOWNED STATESMAN ·

wounded soldiers—Warren to give medical treatment and Vance to cheer them on.

There was a shortage of clothing, leather and food for the soldiers, and the wives and children of the troops were impoverished. Vance, in a proclamation, called upon the people to donate shoes, socks, blankets, shirts and trousers for the troops. There was a dire scarcity of salt required for curing meat; Vance established saltworks along the coast to derive salt from the sea. He arranged to provide food and other needs for destitute widows, wives and children of the soldiers.

The vessels of the Union patrolled the sea at the entrance to Wilmington, the only port in North Carolina, in an effort to blockade ship traffic to and from Wilmington. Upon Vance's call, the General Assembly provided funds to purchase a ship—the name was changed to Ad-Vance—and also interests in other vessels to run the blockade. The ships were successful in running the blockade. They transported cotton and tobacco to Bermuda and then to England in exchange for food, medicine, shoes, clothing, machinery and munitions. The blockade running was crucial to the survival of the Confederacy and to North Carolina. After twelve voyages, the Ad-Vance was captured on January 15, 1865. Fort Fisher was captured by Union forces—as a result Wilmington fell and blockade running ceased, a severe blow to the Confederacy and to North Carolina.

In 1862, when the Norfolk Navy yard was endangered by the approach of the Federal forces, Vance arranged for it to be moved to Charlotte, where it operated for three years on East Trade Street at the railroad—a sign "Confederate States Navy yard 1862–1865" is at that location. It did not build ships; it built fittings, propellers and armament.[23]

Vance was a fervent protector of individual rights. The Confederate Congress had authorized President Davis to suspend the *writ of habeas corpus*. That is a treasured procedure inherited from England—the writ is an order that a prisoner be brought before a court to determine the legality of his detention. Confederate authorities in North Carolina had been imprisoning citizens upon suspicion that they were disloyal to the Confederacy. Vance said if North Carolinians were deprived of the right of *habeas corpus*, "he would issue a proclamation recalling the North Carolina soldiers from Virginia, and call out the State's militia to protect the liberties of the citizens."[24]

Later in a speech, Vance remarked: "The laws were heard amidst the roar of cannon. No man within the jurisdiction of the State of North Carolina was denied the privilege of the *writ of habeas corpus*, the right of trial by jury, or the equal protection of the laws, as provided by our Constitution and the Bill of Rights."[25]

In addition to the complaint about *habeas corpus*, Vance complained frequently to Jefferson Davis—some communications were strident. Carl Sandburg, famous poet and biographer, wrote: "The break between Vance and the Davis Government at Richmond ran deep, the feeling bitter."[26] Lincoln was urged to reach out to Vance and was told, Sandburg wrote, "Vance would welcome reunion of the States and peace compatible with honor. . . . Whether Lincoln . . . convinced Vance that peace efforts would be worthwhile was not clear."[27]

Nevertheless, Vance wrote Davis urging peace negotiations. To send peace proposals was, Davis responded, "to invite insult and contumely, and to subject ourselves to indignity without the slightest chance of being listened to," and further, "I fear much, from the tenor of the news I receive from North Carolina, that an attempt will be made by some bad men to inaugurate movements which must be considered as equivalent to aid and comfort to the enemy, and which all patriots should combine to put down at any cost."[28]

William W. Holden, the avid supporter of the election of Vance in 1862 and editor of *The Weekly Standard*, launched a movement for North Carolina to enter into negotiations with the Union for a separate peace. Vance favored peace, but only in coordination with the Confederacy. Vance wrote that the seeking of a separate peace would "steep the name of North Carolina in infamy . . ." and that he would ". . . see Holden in hell . . . before he would consent to a separate peace."[29]

Vance decided to run for a second term. Holden announced as Vance's opponent. The election was held on August 4, 1864—the governor's term then was two years. Vance campaigned throughout the State—a speech in Wilmington lasted for two and one-half hours. As part of his response to Holden's demand for a separate peace, Vance remarked that he told the troops to "fight till hell froze over and then fight on the ice."[30] Vance defeated Holden overwhelmingly. Vance's formidable speaking ability won the day.

As previously noted, on January 15, 1865, Fort Fisher fell and thereafter Wilmington was occupied by Union troops. This was an ominous event for North Carolina and the Confederacy. Later, the Union forces under the command of General William Tecumseh Sherman conquered the eastern counties and were approaching Raleigh —110,000 men strong. The subjugation of the State Capitol was imminent. Vance transferred records and military equipment to the western part of the State. Vance had previously sent his family to Statesville for greater security. On April 11, Vance received a message that General Lee had surrendered to Grant at Appomattox. On April 12 Vance sent his close friends and former governors, Graham and Swain, as emissaries to General Sherman for terms under which Vance could remain in Raleigh to conduct affairs of government and to request protection of Raleigh. His emissaries were delayed in returning, and at midnight Vance departed Raleigh on horseback to General Robert Hoke's encampment—a Confederate camp. Jefferson Davis invited

Vance to meet him in Greensboro where the Confederate Cabinet was meeting; when Vance arrived in Greensboro he learned that Davis and his cabinet had moved to Charlotte on April 19. Vance followed and met with Davis at the Bank of North Carolina at 122 South Tryon Street. Davis suggested that the remains of the Confederate Army retreat beyond the Mississippi, and proposed that Vance accompany him with the North Carolina troops. Davis was discouraged and this idea was dropped. While in Charlotte, Davis received word that Abraham Lincoln had been assassinated. Vance bid Davis farewell, and after further stops and meetings, proceeded to Statesville to be with his family.

The Confederate Army in North Carolina, under the command of General Joseph E. Johnston, on April 18 surrendered to General Sherman.

Sherman and his army arrived in Raleigh on April 13. The Confederate flag on the Capitol was lowered and the stars and stripes were hoisted. Sherman made the Governor's mansion his temporary headquarters. His troops marched up Fayetteville Street and Sherman watched them in review at the Capitol.[31]

Professor Frontis W. Johnston wrote about Vance:

> His career as War Governor is more responsible than any other thing for the fact that North Carolina has loved, idolized, and rewarded no other man in her history as she has Zebulon Baird Vance.[32]

On May 11, 1865, General Ulysses S. Grant issued an order to Major General J. M. Schofield, Commander of Union Forces in North Carolina: "By direction of the President [Andrew Johnson] you will at once arrest Zebulon B. Vance, late Rebel Governor of North Carolina."

On May 13, 1865, Vance's home at Statesville was surrounded by about three hundred Federal cavalry and Vance was placed under arrest. Vance was escorted to the train station at Salisbury and then to Washington where he was incarcerated in the Old Capitol Prison. He was not charged with any criminal violation, just taken to jail. Vance was granted a parole and released from prison on July 6, 1865, on condition that he remain in North Carolina (unless permission granted to travel further) subject to President Johnson's further orders. Later President Johnson, a native of North Carolina and acquaintance of Vance, issued a full pardon.

"THE SCATTERED NATION"

"The Scattered Nation" was acclaimed as Vance's greatest lecture.

The thrust of "The Scattered Nation" was an ardent appeal for friendship with the Jewish people. Vance said: ". . . there remains among us an unreasonable prejudice of which I am heartily ashamed. Our toleration will not be complete until we put it away. . . ." And further: ". . . I consider it a grave reproach not only to us, but to all Christendom that such injustice is permitted anywhere."[33]

The date on which "The Scattered Nation" was first delivered and the number of years over which it was delivered appear to be uncertain. Franklin Ray Shirley, Professor at Wake Forest University, in 1962, wrote: "Vance's greatest lecture, 'The Scattered Nation' was delivered for the first time on February 13, 1874. . . . It seems certain that over a period of fifteen years 'The Scattered Nation' was delivered hundreds of times and in almost every important city in the United States.[34]

On the other hand, Selig Adler found "internal evidence within" that the speech would indicate that it was written between 1868 and 1873, and that it was delivered over "fifteen to twenty years."

Vance prepared "The Scattered Nation" while practicing law in Charlotte; his roll-top desk is on display at the Vance Museum at Reems Creek Valley; on the desk is a sign stating that "The Scattered Nation" was prepared on this desk.

The Charlotte and South Carolina Railroad arrived in Charlotte in 1852, and the Vance family lived along the tracks at 6th Street—with the porch facing the railroad. Vance and his wife, Harriett, and their four sons, Charles, David, Zebulon, Jr. and Thomas, attended the First Presbyterian Church on West Trade Street—a bronze plaque, with his name on it, is still on their pew. He was not an adherent of the Presbyterian Church until later in life.

As noted previously, Vance was famous for using anecdotes and humor, but in "The Scattered Nation" he was completely serious and solemn.

Of course, during Vance's days, there was no television, radio nor motion-picture theaters. Lyceums were popular—a hall in which lectures and concerts were presented. Vance drew crowds for the speech because of his fame as a lecturer, and the title of the lecture aroused curiosity.

In the speech he revealed his scholarship, and his keen knowledge of Jewish history and the Bible; and he referred to the writings of Tacitus, Socrates, Josephus, Macaulay and Machiavelli. As a busy lawyer, it is remarkable that he found time to prepare this outstanding speech.

Important questions arise: What inspired Vance to extol Judaism and the Jews when others were defaming or silent? What motivated Vance to prepare and deliver "The Scattered Nation"? What impelled Vance to travel to many distant cities, and deliver the oration to numerous audiences? These queries arose in the mind of Dr. Selig Adler, Distinguished Professor of History at the University of Buffalo. Over fifty years ago, in 1939, he came to North Carolina to search for the answers. Adler engaged in extensive research: he visited Charlotte, Asheville, Statesville, Raleigh, and Chapel Hill; he conferred with people, still living, who knew Vance; he read old newspaper clippings at the University of North Carolina, and he read much of Vance's correspondence at the archives of the North Carolina Division of Archives and History. He then wrote an essay that was published in *The Journal of Southern History* in 1941 entitled "Zebulon B. Vance and 'The Scattered Nation.'"[35] His article is republished in this book as Chapter Two. Adler answers the above questions in a fascinating essay.

Vance in his oration said the Jews are to be found ". . . in almost all of the cities of the globe. . . ." What caused this scattering from which the speech takes its title? Vance says the Jewish people suffered "in the fiercest fires of human cruelty, though heated seven times in the furnace of religious bigotry. . . ."[36] The migrations from Europe were principally caused by that "cruelty" and "religious bigotry." Then, what caused the "cruelty" and the "religious bigotry"?

The theology of Christianity taught that the destruction of the Second Temple by Rome in the year 70 and the dispersal of the Jews were punishment for rejection of the divinity of Jesus; that Christianity was the fulfillment of Judaism; that the Church is the one true chosen people of God; that the Church was the new Israel; that Christianity was heir to the Covenant between God and Abraham; and that Jews were identified with the devil and their synagogues were the abodes of satan.

Clark M. Williamson, Professor at the Christian Theological Seminary, wrote: "A torrent of anti-Judaism flows through the channels of Christianity."[37]

Words and concepts have serious consequences; in Europe, especially in medieval days, they resulted in forced conversions of Jews, denigrations, persecutions, book burnings, defamations, restrictions, the Inquisition and murder.

In the Middle Ages, the Dominicans and the Franciscans were in the vanguard in anti-Jewish and anti-Judaism activity.

> . . . Dominican and Franciscan friars directed and oversaw virtually all of the anti-Jewish activities of the Chris-

tian clergy in the West. As inquisitors, missionaries, disputants, polemicists, scholars, and itinerant preachers, mendicants engaged in concerted efforts to undermine the religious freedom and physical security of the medieval Jewish community . . . and who actively promoted hatred among the laity of Western Christendom.[38]

Many Jews fled, scattered by impoverishment and oppression to places with a measure of opportunity and freedom. A greater number were expelled as church and states sought to homogenize their populations—uniformity of religious thought. For examples: England expelled the Jews in 1290 and they were not permitted to return until 1650 —during the days of Oliver Cromwell. In an enormous expulsion, Spain drove the Jews out in 1492; and most of the countries of Central and Western Europe did the same. It was "an ethnic and religious cleansing."

Beginning in 1880, during Vance's time, there were pogroms in Russia (officially encouraged massacres and persecutions). Vance refers to this in a later version of "The Scattered Nation." The oppression grew intense in Eastern Europe, causing substantial migration—"scattering"—to the United States, Canada, Argentina, South Africa, Australia and other places in the world.

This sordid history has been depicted by scholars, both Christian and Jewish, in many volumes—here we present a summary.[39] Also, many scholars have referred to the events of this history as precursors of the Holocaust. James Parkes, the British clergyman and historian has written: "This hatred and denigration have a quite clear and precise historical origin. They arise from Christian preaching and teaching from the time of the bitter controversies of the first century in which the two religions separated from each other. From that time up to today there has been an unbroken line which culminates in the massacre in our own day of six million Jews."[40]

Preceding and after the Holocaust, Jews were further

"scattered." Before the Holocaust, many escaped the Nazi regime by going to what later became the State of Israel, and some escaped during the Holocaust. Many were unable to reach Israel because the British imposed a blockade of Israel to please the Arabs; some ended up in distant places, as far away as Shanghai.

There was another substantial "scattering" when about seven hundred thousand Jews fled or were expelled from the Arab countries after the State of Israel defeated the Arabs who committed aggression against Israel in 1948, 1967 and 1973. Islam taught that Jews and Christians were to be humiliated and made subservient; they were called *dhimmis*. Therefore, the loss of the Arab-Israel wars at the hands of those to be humiliated caused shock and trauma in the Arab world; the status of Jews became extremely precarious.

In 1965, the Vatican Council II declared in *Nostra Aetate* (In Our Time) that the Church "deplores hatred, persecutions, and displays of anti-Semitism directed against Jews at any time from any source." And further: "Jews should not be presented as rejected or accursed by God. ..."

Many Protestant denominations have issued similar laudatory statements.

During recent years, about five hundred thousand Jews have migrated from the States of the former Soviet Union to the State of Israel. This emigration has been caused by continued hostility toward Jews, enhanced by economic adversity and political turmoil. So, the migrations have continued for over a century after Vance's "The Scattered Nation."

JEWISH TRIBUTES

Vance's "The Scattered Nation" and his delivery of the speech in many cities was unique. This made a profound impression on the Jewish community of North Carolina and elsewhere. They expressed their admiration for his kind words in many ways.

Selig Adler in his article, published in 1941, relates: "Each May 13, Vance's birthday, the Asheville representatives of the United Daughters of the Confederacy and B'nai B'rith sponsor a program around the Vance monument." That statement was made by Adler over fifty years ago. Inquiry was recently made by this writer, and it was determined that the ceremony has continued to the present day, except that during the past few years it has been held at Vance's birthplace at Reems Creek Valley.

Adler also talks of the visit of Nathan Straus of New York, who visited Asheville and placed a wreath at the Vance obelisk. Straus was a merchandising magnate (R.H. Macy & Company) and prolific philanthropist. He provided funds for erection of a wrought iron fence around the base of the monument, and established an endowment for a wreath to be placed at the Vance monument every year.

In 1926 the Central Conference of American Rabbis held a convention in Asheville. They assembled at Riverside Cemetery and placed a wreath on Vance's grave.[41]

Glenn Tucker wrote: "When he delivered in Chapel Hill . . . his most famous lecture, 'The Scattered Nation,' a number of North Carolina Jews presented him with a gold-headed cane."[42]

The State of North Carolina built and maintains a museum adjacent to the log cabin in which Vance was born at Reems Creek Valley. In it are memorabilia of Vance's life such as his pistol and sword. Among the items is a silver-headed cane inscribed: "Presented to Zebulon B. Vance by the Jewish youth of Wilmington."

The Calvary Episcopal Church established in 1859, at Fletcher, North Carolina,[43] has sponsored the erection of monuments on the church grounds in honor and memory of outstanding southern personalities. Among them are

Francis Scott Key, James Whitcomb Riley, and Stephen C. Foster. On October 14, 1928, a monument was dedicated to the memory of Zebulon B. Vance under the patronage of B'nai B'rith of Asheville. Nathan Straus sent a message: "As a Southerner and in common with all American Jews I join in the tribute of gratitude and affection to the memory of North Carolina's great Senator and war governor. . . . 'The Scattered Nation' will never be forgotten."

The principal speaker was Rabbi Stephen S. Wise of New York, the preeminent rabbi in America at the time. Wise said: "Mine is a people which enshrines memories older than those of any other people . . . Senator Vance, not by any act of ours but by his own imperishable word has enshrined his name on the roll of the unforgettable. . . . It must be that the passion of human brotherhood inspired the words of Vance."[44]

GOVERNOR AGAIN

While Vance was practicing law in Charlotte, the convention of the Democratic Party, on June 14, 1876, nominated him to be Governor of North Carolina for the third time. In the interim, the Conservative Party had changed its name to the Democratic Party.

Upon his return from the convention in Raleigh a celebration was held in Charlotte:

> Handbills announcing a meeting to be held in Independence Square were printed and distributed throughout the city. Long before the arrival of the 9:20 p.m. train, which was bringing Vance from Raleigh, tar barrels were set on fire and throngs of people gathered in the streets waiting to hear what their distinguished townsman had to say about his nomination. A large delegation was waiting at the depot when the train pulled in, and the popular candidate was hurried into a waiting carriage, which was

pulled by four grey horses to the Square. As the carriage came in sight a band began playing, and shouts of "hurrah for Vance" echoed through the air.

Amid thunderous applause, Vance mounted the platform which was illuminated by blazing tar barrels. He was introduced to the crowd as "North Carolina's favorite son," the tribune of the people, Zebulon B. Vance.[45]

Vance's opponent, representing the Republican Party, was Thomas Settle, a former member of the North Carolina Supreme Court and a formidable candidate. The election was referred to as "the battle of the giants."[46] It was an extensive, hard-fought campaign.

Vance "spoke in Burgaw in the afternoon for two and a half hours, and then taking an extra train for Wilmington . . . he again spoke for two and a half hours."[47] In the three months of the campaign, he delivered sixty-nine speeches in sixty-five counties.[48] Many of the addresses by Vance were in debates with Settle.

As usual Vance's lectures were replete with humor; for example, when jesting about revenue officers he said they "could lie down and drink out of a branch and tell if there was a still five miles up it, and could look at a man's track and tell whether he was toting a quart of whiskey or a two gallon jug."[49]

Vance won the election by a vote of 118,000 to Settle's 104,000. He delivered his third inaugural address as Governor of North Carolina on January 1, 1877—it implicitly marked the end of the era of Reconstruction.

During the campaign, Vance advocated the supremacy of the white race, and that "this supremacy would never pass to alien blood with his consent;"[50] that position was the prevalent view in the populace. Vance's point of view, in that respect, was ameliorated by his deep concern for improvement of education—universal education.

Soon after the inauguration, he delivered a message to the General Assembly calling for equal education for both races—then, equal meant separate. Vance urged the legislature to establish two normal schools, one for African-American teachers, and one for the white race, to improve abilities of the teachers. He said, "It is impossible for the blind to lead the blind." And further that a school for the "education of colored teachers, the want of which is more deeply felt by the black race even than the white." The General Assembly complied, and the Fayetteville Colored Normal School and the white school at Chapel Hill were established.

In 1878, in an address to an African-American audience, he said that although he had opposed emancipation, he would "respect all the rights the laws had invested in them." This, he said, "I cheerfully do, always have done, and always shall do."[51]

In 1886, while a United States Senator, in a speech in Boston, Vance remarked: ". . . slavery has been forever abolished, no longer to tarnish the fair fame of this great free Republic."[52]

Vance was a keen advocate of vocational education—training for industry and agriculture. He referred to a liberal arts education as "ornamental education." His theme, in speeches, was "providing an ornamental education to the exclusion of a practical one might prove disastrous to the state."[53]

From time to time, during this term as Governor, Vance continued to deliver "The Scattered Nation."

At the end of 1878, the General Assembly elected Vance to the United States Senate by acclamation to succeed Senator A. S. Merriman whose term had expired.[54] On March 4, 1879, he reported to Washington and became a United States Senator.

UNITED STATES SENATOR

In the Senate, Vance was a diligent student of the issues of the times; his speeches were well-prepared and erudite.

As in the past, his concepts were illustrated with jokes and anecdotes, accompanied by wisdom.

Reminiscent of the days in Charlotte when crowds came to hear him in court, in the Senate, when it was known in advance that he would speak, the galleries were full.

The Philadelphia Times reported: ". . . the fascination of his fun is in its spontaneity, its originality and the inexhaustible fecundity of the imagination which generates it. His mind is a vast reservoir of humor. . . ."[55]

He was swift with repartee. Listen to this: "I heard your speech," a colleague remarked tauntingly one day, "but it went in one ear and out the other."

"Nothing to stop it," was Vance's quick reply.[56]

Vance was heard to remark: "Mirth does for the soul what sleep does for the body."[57]

During recesses, he accepted invitations to address audiences all over the nation: college commencements, boards of trade, historical societies, and veterans organizations. He also continued to deliver "The Scattered Nation."

In 1882, Vance returned to Charlotte to introduce Senator Thomas F. Bayard of Delaware, a leader in the Senate, as the principal speaker on the anniversary of the Mecklenburg Declaration of Independence. Vance, in part, said, "We have met to worship once again at the shrine of American liberty, upon the spot where it was born."[58]

In 1892, Vance returned again to Charlotte to deliver an address. *The Charlotte Observer* reported: ". . . and such an expression of love, affection and esteem was never shown to any son of North Carolina at any time, or anywhere, as was expressed in the great ovation over Vance." Vance commented, in part: "It makes me glad at heart to see such an audience in Mecklenburg, and to make you a speech is as tempting to me as a good dinner would be to a real hungry man."[59]

In a speech in 1880 in opposition to the Republican's proposed budget, he said: "If I thought the Republican

Party were standing upon the brink of a precipice, beneath which seethed those cold waters of oblivion, instead of warning them, I pledge you my word I would try to induce them to step over the edge; in fact, I might lend them a push." [laughter][60]

Among Vance's chief concerns were tariff, silver and the civil service. He favored elimination of tariff on commodities purchased by all the people.[61] President Grover Cleveland, in 1885, advocated the cessation of silver coinage. Vance vehemently favored bimetallism, continuation of silver coinage. On the civil service issue, Vance advocated repeal of the Civil Service Act so that when a President is elected with a change in party there be no limitation on patronage. Vance remarked: "I believe most earnestly that parties are indispensable to the existence of liberty, and that government by the party is the only way in which there can be government by the people."[62]

Inspired by his love for the mountains of North Carolina where he was born and reared, he bought and improved a Victorian mansion near Black Mountain, about 22 miles from Asheville. He called it Gombroon. It was here that he relaxed when the Senate was not in session and when he was not delivering speeches.

He was reelected to the United States Senate in 1885, and again in 1891.

During his terms in the Senate the Presidents were Rutherford B. Hayes, James A. Garfield, Chester A. Arthur, Grover Cleveland, and Benjamin Harrison.

While in the Senate, Vance was a magnificent representative of North Carolina, was looked upon as the spokesman of the South and was deeply concerned about the welfare of the nation.

OUTPOURING OF GRIEF

Vance passed away on April 14, 1894, in his third term in the United States Senate. There was an enormous outpouring of grief. A memorial ceremony held in Congress was attended by President Grover Cleveland, Vice President Adlai Stevenson (grandfather of Adlai Stevenson, who ran for President in 1952 and 1956), the Cabinet, the Supreme Court, diplomats and members of the Senate and House.

The funeral train, with delegations from the Senate and House of Representatives abroad, traveled to Raleigh where a procession escorted the casket to the Capitol. The hearse was pulled by four black horses. It was most appropriate to visit the Capitol where Vance had served the people of North Carolina for three terms as Governor. Then, en route to Asheville, the funeral train stopped at Durham and Greensboro where throngs awaited, bands played sacred music, choirs sang hymns, flags were flown at half mast, buildings were draped in black and church bells tolled. "At Asheville, a procession of ten thousand people, both military and civilian, escorted the casket to Riverside Cemetery for the final rites and interment."[63]

Across North Carolina, in cities and towns, memorial services were held. In Charlotte, a memorial ceremony was held on the day before the funeral and another a day after; prominent Charlotte citizens delivered eulogies. Reports of each of the memorial ceremonies in Charlotte are in Appendices A and B.[64]

However, the accolades did not cease with the funeral; the plaudits and commemorations continued for many years.

On January 19, 1895, an additional memorial ceremony was held in the United States Senate. Nine Senators delivered eulogies; the principal one was delivered by Senator Matt W. Ransom, Vance's colleague from North Carolina. It was a magnificent address. Excerpts from the Ransom eulogy are in Appendix C.[65]

On August 22, 1900, a bronze statue of Vance was

erected on the grounds of the Capitol at Raleigh. He stands robust, and, appropriately, with a hand on a book; and on each side are quotations from his speeches engraved in bronze. Excerpts from dedicatory address by Kemp H. Battle are in Appendix D.[66]

In 1916, a bronze statue of Vance was unveiled in Statuary Hall of the Capitol in Washington; the sculptor was the famous Gutzan Borglum. In 1864 Congress enacted a law inviting each State to furnish statues, not exceeding two of its citizens "illustrious for their historic renown." The North Carolina Legislature unanimously authorized a statue of Vance to be placed in Statuary Hall. In the ceremonies, addresses were delivered in Statuary Hall and also in the Senate and House of Representatives. Among the stirring addresses was one by Locke Craig, Governor of North Carolina. Excerpts from his speech are in Appendix E.[67]

In 1898 a tall obelisk, in memory of Vance, was dedicated on Pack Square in Asheville. Excerpts from the address by R. L. Taylor, Governor of Tennessee, are in Appendix F.[68]

The appendices are important: They present excerpts of speeches by Vance's distinguished colleagues and are replete with historical events in the life of Vance.

The General Assembly selected another of its illustrious citizens to be honored with a statue in Statuary Hall: Charles B. Aycock, Governor from 1901 to 1905, who was also famous for encouraging education.

Throughout North Carolina, towns and cities named streets and schools in memory of Vance. Vance County was named in honor of him during his lifetime. At the turn of the century, "more sons, dogs, horses and mules were named Zeb than any other name, largely in affectionate tribute to Zebulon Baird Vance, the most beloved man ever elected to public office in the State."[69]

The people of North Carolina mourned and wept for

their renowned statesman who had been their magnificent leader, in war and peace, for one third of a century. Above all, the people knew that Zebulon B. Vance was a compassionate statesman who always spoke the truth.

NOTES TO CHAPTER ONE

ELOQUENCE

1. From speech by Locke Craig, Governor of North Carolina at the dedication of statue of Zebulon B. Vance in Statuary Hall, U.S. Capitol, 1916.

2. Schenck diary, November 2, 1874, University of North Carolina.

3. Ashe, Samuel, editor, *History of North Carolina* II (Greensboro, 1907), p. 880.

4. Warren, Edward, *A Doctor's Experiences in Three Continents*, (Baltimore, 1885), p. 314.

5. Shirley, Franklin Ray, *Zebulon Vance, Tarheel Spokesman* (Charlotte, 1962), p. 139.

6. *Ibid.*, p. 3.

7. Tucker, Glenn, *Zeb Vance, Champion of Personal Freedom* (Indianapolis, 1965), p. 21.

8. Address by Z. B. Vance to graduating class of Wake Forest College (Raleigh, 1872), p. 15.

HERITAGE

9. Johnston, Frontis W., *Zebulon B. Vance Letters* (State Department of Archives and History, Raleigh, 1963), p. xx.

POLITICAL CAREER LAUNCHED

10. Address of Richard H. Battle in *Literary and Historical Activities in North Carolina* (Raleigh, 1907), p. 381.

11. *Ibid.*, p. 383.

12. *Ibid.*, p. 383.

13. Johnston, p. xxxvi.

14. Dowd, Clement, *Life of Zebulon Vance* (Charlotte, 1897), p. 44.

15. Tucker, p. 88.

16. Shirley, p. 22.

17. Tucker, p. 105.

18. Barrett, John G., *The Civil War in North Carolina* (Chapel Hill, 1963), p. 12.

19. *Ibid.*, p. 12.

20. Johnston, p. xi.

THE WAR GOVERNOR

21. Tucker, p. 149.

22. *Raleigh Register*, September 10, 1862.

23. Tucker, p. 179.
24. Letter of protest to Jefferson Davis, July 6, 1863. Vance Letter Book Vol. I, p. 317.
25. Vance address to Grand Army of the Republic, Boston, December 8, 1876. Dowd, p. 453.
26. Sandburg, Carl, *Abraham Lincoln: The War Years*, Vol. II (New York, 1939), p. 392.
27. *Ibid.*, Vol. II, p. 393.
28. *Ibid.*, Vol. III, p. 156.
29. Letter – Vance to David Swain, Raleigh, January 2, 1864, Vance Papers.
30. Johnston, p. lxvii.
31. Spencer, Cornelia P., *The Last Ninety Days of the War in North Carolina* (New York, 1866), p. 138.
32. Johnston, p. lxxiii.

"THE SCATTERED NATION"

33. "The Scattered Nation" — Chapter Three, p. 61.
34. Shirley, p. 122.
35. *The Southern Journal of History*, Vol. VIII, No. 3. August, 1941. Chapter Two in this volume, p. 35.
36. Vance, Chapter Three, p. 61.
37. Williamson, Clark M., *Has God Rejected His People? Anti-Judaism in the Christian Church* (Nashville, 1982), p. 100.
38. Cohen, Jeremy, *The Friars and the Jews* (Ithaca, 1982), p. 13.
39. See: Berger, David, ed., *History and Hate* (Philadelphia, 1986).
Williamson, Clark, *Has God Rejected His People?* (Nashville, 1982).
Littell, Franklin H., *The Crucifixion of the Jews* (New York, 1975).
Eckardt, A. Roy, *Elder and Younger Brothers* (New York, 1973).
Boksor, Ben Zion, *Judaism and the Christian Predicament* (New York, 1967).
Isaac, Jules, *The Teaching of Contempt* (New York, 1964).
40. Parkes, James, *The Conflict of Church and Synagogue* (Cleveland, 1961).

JEWISH TRIBUTES

41. Central Conference of American Rabbis Year Book, Vol. 36 (1926), p. 17.
42. Tucker, p. 454.
43. In his article, Chapter Two, Selig Adler wrote that this event took place in Asheville: That was an error. The event took place in Fletcher, North Carolina.
44. *The Asheville Times*, October 15, 1928, p. 12.

GOVERNOR AGAIN

45. Shirley, p. 72. Quoted from *The Charlotte Democrat* of June 19, 1876.
46. Dowd, p. 146.
47. Vance Papers, Raleigh. Clipping Book, p. 2351.

48. Dowd, p. 161.
49. *Ibid.*, p. 150.
50. *Raleigh Sentinel*, July 15, 1876.
51. Shirley, p. 88.
52. Dowd, p. 453.
53. Shirley, pp. 90–91.
54. Amendment XVII to the United States Constitution, adopted May 31, 1913, provided for direct popular election of United States Senators.

United States Senator

55. *Raleigh Observer*, April 9, 1879.
56. Tucker, p. 466.
57. *Ibid.*, p. 465.
58. Tucker, pp. 466–467.
59. Dowd, pp. 256–257.
60. Dowd, p. 238.
61. Until 1913, tariffs were the principal sources of revenue. The XVI Amendment to the Constitution authorized income taxes.
62. Cong. Record, 49th Congress, 1st Session, p. 2945.

Outpouring of Grief

63. Dowd, p. 316.
64. See appendix for reports of the two memorial ceremonies in Charlotte, pp. 97 and 100.
65. See appendix for excerpts from eulogy by Senator Matt W. Ransom, p. 105.
66. See appendix for excerpts from dedicatory address by Richard H. Battle, p. 114.
67. See appendix for excerpts from address by Governor Locke Craig, p. 123.
68. See appendix for excerpts from address by R. L. Taylor, Governor of Tennessee, p. 130.
69. Claiborne, Jack, and William Price, editors, *Discovering North Carolina*, Essay by Richard Walser (Chapel Hill, 1991), p. 132.

Zebulon Vance
and
"The Scattered Nation"

CHAPTER TWO

Zebulon Vance
and
"The Scattered Nation"

BY SELIG ADLER

1941

The American Civil War raised many men from obscurity to state and national prominence. Almost every state, North and South, had its latter nineteenth-century hero. With the exception of those whose roles were so important as to incorporate their deeds into the everyday knowledge of the average citizen, they have been forgotten. There is, however, one of this group whose memory still lives within his own state, whose stories are still told, whose name is still meaningful. That person is Zebulon Baird Vance, who followed the *cursus honorum* in North Carolina from county attorney to the General Assembly to two terms in the lower house of Congress, from a colonel in the Confederate army to a great southern war governor. Eleven years after Appomattox he returned to the governor's chair at Raleigh, according to a southern verdict, to deliver "his people of the Old North State from the bonds of oppression and from the Egypt of reconstruction."[1] From the governorship Vance went to the Senate where he died in his third elective term.

Although Vance has been dead forty-seven years, his memory is still alive. His monument on Capitol Square, Raleigh, is the only statue ever erected by public funds in the history of the state.[2] In 1916 his name was chosen to represent North Carolina in the National Hall of Statuary in Washington. The newspapers still mention him; his jokes are a part of the folklore of the state; intimate knowledge of his doings still persists. The salient facts of Vance's career and character explain this unusual devotion and tribute. Born in the mountain country near Asheville in 1830, by his thirtieth birthday Vance was a state-wide figure serving his second term in Congress. He was an ardent Unionist at first, but the firing on Fort Sumter led him into the secessionist camp. In 1862, while gaining a reputation for gallantry on the field of battle and maintaining unusual morale with his anecdotes and jokes, he was elected governor of the state. As war governor, Vance endeared himself forever to his people. He mitigated the horrors of war by insisting on the precedence of civil law, and stoutly protected the state from the uncomfortable militarism of the Confederate government. Despite his differences with President Jefferson Davis, Vance fought the fight to the end, leaving Raleigh on the advance of William T. Sherman's army in April, 1865. After an unsatisfactory conference with Davis at Charlotte, he surrendered himself to the Federal forces. General John M. Schofield told him to proceed to his home at Statesville and there to await further orders. While in Statesville he made his first intimate acquaintance with the members of a people who treasure his memory equally with his own kith and kin. To North Carolinians he is the incomparable Vance of war and Senate fame and many jests; to the Jewish people he is the author of the "Scattered Nation," the one American statesman of his day who pleaded their cause to the people of the United States.

Vance arrived in Statesville early in May, 1865. There

and later in Charlotte he came into close contact with a number of Jewish merchants whose friendship served to inspire the "Scattered Nation."[3] The leading mercantile establishment of the town was Wallace Brothers and Stephenson. Isaac and David Wallace were typical German-Jewish immigrants of the mid-century. In 1859, after peddling and keeping store in the vicinity of Bamberg, South Carolina, they moved to Statesville. From the first they took a leading part in the affairs of this farming metropolis of six hundred souls. Their general store was the hub center of county and trading gossip. They sold supplies to the farmers, ran a small banking business as an accommodation, and even included a drug counter. From the handling of standard home remedies they came upon an idea which has benefited that section of the state for seventy-five years. The farmers of Wilkes, Ashe, and Watauga counties had thus far not capitalized upon the variety of herbs found in their farmyards. The Wallaces taught them to bring goldenseal root, ginseng, black haw, and eventually some six hundred other varieties of roots and herbs into Statesville in return for merchandise.[4] This was the beginning of a crude drug business which still continues to be a source of prosperity to the local countryside.

The visits of Vance to the country store are recalled to this day. There was much about Isaac and David Wallace to impress the war Governor. They were, in the language of the present oldest inhabitant of Statesville, the "substantial people of the town," men of integrity and foresight. They were liberal in their terms to struggling small landowners and generous donors to worthwhile causes.[5] Realizing that they were an isolated minority, they were ultraconsiderate of the feelings of their Gentile neighbors. Their integrity of character was well appreciated. The minister of the First Presbyterian Church, which the Vances attended, was the Wallaces' friend. With their neighbors, the family had struggled through the long war years. A detachment of Union men foraged the Wallace home during Passover, 1865. Failing to find bread, they sampled the unleavened cakes of the season to whirl them through the air with the disgruntled comment of "more hard tack."[6] This incident occurred shortly before Vance returned to Statesville under General Schofield's orders.

The Governor was allowed but short respite with his family. On May 13, 1865, which chanced to be his thirty-fifth birthday, a squadron of General Hugh J. Kilpatrick's cavalry surrounded his home, arrested him, and prepared to take him to Washington. As the railroad and telegraph lines had been destroyed, Statesville was completely cut off from the outside world. The Union officer in charge wanted the Governor to ride horseback thirty-five miles to the railroad at Salisbury. There being some question as to the corpulent Zeb's equestrian abilities, a Jewish resident agreed to drive him by buggy to Salisbury. This man was destined to become one of the most enterprising and successful men in the state and was probably the most intimate of Vance's Jewish friends. He was Samuel Wittkowsky who had been born in 1835 in Prussian Poland. Arriving in New York at the age of eighteen with but $3.00 in gold, he had worked his way upward in various places in the South, and during the war had been engaged in the manufacture of hats in Statesville in the firm of Wittkowsky and Saltzgiver. He had probably long admired Vance, for early in 1865 he sent him a "black hat of our make."[7] Thus on that May day of 1865 the famous war Governor and the immigrant Jew started out on the long buggy ride to Salisbury surrounded by two hundred Federal cavalrymen.

Wittkowsky was fond of recalling that ride in later years. He often told how Vance turned to him, wiped the tears from his cheeks, and said: "This will not do. I must be a man, but I am not so much concerned as to what may be in store for me, but my poor wife and little children—they have not a cent of money—and my poor State—what indignity may be in store for her?"[8] As they rode on, however, Vance's naturally good spirits returned, and by the time they reached Salisbury he had so charmed the Yankees with his stories that they spared him the indignity of riding into town an obvious prisoner. Thus began his intimate acquaintance with a Jew whose slogan "Push, Pluck and Perseverance" was to make him a leading and valuable citizen of Charlotte, a city in which he and Vance were often to meet.

In Washington, on May 20, 1865, Vance was consigned to Old Capitol Prison. Vance's efforts to soften the horrors of war and to care for Federal prisoners soon came to the attention of the irascible Secretary of War, Edwin M. Stanton. On July 6 the Governor was paroled within the limits of North Carolina, Stanton saying to him, " 'Upon your record you stand acquitted.' "[9] Vance spent the next six months in weighing the possibilities of Wilmington and Charlotte as opportune cities for the practice of law. Confidence in Charlotte's future and absence of serious legal competition there were responsible for his decision in favor of that city.

Charlotte had just received its city charter and, in 1866, boasted of some three thousand inhabitants. Vance was destined to spend ten years in this pleasant little city which was to become the most thriving community in the state before the turn of the century. His genial personality radiated through the streets of the town; his appearances in court "became gala occasions" during which the populace suspended business.[10] The Attorney's popularity and availability soon brought him political honors almost without effort on his part. On November 29, 1870, the legislature elected him United States senator. The cinders of war, however, had not yet cooled sufficiently to allow so important an ex-Confederate to have a voice in the upper council of the nation. The Republican Senate refused to seat him, and he settled down to six more years of the law. When these were over he was to be in public service for the rest of his life.

Vance's Charlotte years brought him into intimate acquaintance with a number of Jewish merchants. The concentration of Jewish stores in the proximity of his law office afforded opportunities for daily close contact. More than one good Vance story must have had its first telling in the "merchantile establishments" which lined the center of the town. The great majority of Charlotte Jews was of German origin. They were the young, able, and enterprising part of German Jewry who probably left Europe because of the attractions of the New World rather than the persecutions of the Old. The combination of a good secular education, nineteenth-century German liberalism, and good business sense made for solid citizenship. The Jewish community in Charlotte dated from the early 1850's. "When the railroad got to town the merchants multiplied," wrote the county historian. "Ready-made clothing first made its appearance with the advent of Levi Drucker. The Israelites followed close on the coming of the railroads. They have proved amongst our best citizens."[11] The small Jewish settlement took an active part in the war. In 1861 the Jewish women raised $150 to assist the volunteers and were commended for their interest.[12] The Charlotte Grays marched to war with E. B. Cohen as first lieutenant, and there was a fair sprinkling of Jewish names in the muster roll of the First North Carolina Regiment which was enlisted in Charlotte in 1861.[13] With the end of the war, Jewish mercantile establishments multiplied. Vance's Statesville friend, Wittkowsky, moved to Charlotte and with Jacob Rintels re-established the prewar firm of Wittkowsky and Rintels. The partners rented a room twenty-one feet square, bought some old, rough planking, and put up the calico-covered shelving themselves.[14] In the 1880's Wittkowsky turned to pioneering in the cotton mill industry in the vicinity of Charlotte. From the sale of cotton mill stock on weekly payment terms of twenty-five cents a share, he organized in 1883 the Mechanics Perpetual Building and Loan Association, which is today the second largest organization of its kind in the state. In his last years Wittkowsky was president of the North Carolina Building and Loan League, and today he is recognized as the father of that type of enterprise in the Upper South. In 1902 the Charlotte *News and Times Democrat* called him the city's most useful citizen although "not only an adopted citizen of his present home, but a native of a foreign land."[15]

Vance, admittedly improvident in his own affairs, admired Wittkowsky's contributions to the state's enterprises. But the direct extent of Wittkowsky's influence on Vance's Jewish interests is conjectural. An estimate of this influence must be discounted by the fact that Wittkowsky is remembered today as an assimilationist with few Jewish interests. He did, however, state publicly at the time of Vance's death:

> I speak for my race in North Carolina—aye for my people of the whole Union. The deceased has ever by his words and writings demonstrated that he was their friend. His lecture on the Scattered Nation will ever remain green in the memory of my race, and will be one of the brightest jewels to his ever liberal, fair and untarnished escutcheon. And I venture here the assertion that in the history of North Carolina no Israelite has cast a vote against Z. B. Vance.[16]

Samuel Wittkowksy was the most intimate, but not by any means the only one of Vance's Jewish friends. Strolling along the sunny streets of downtown Charlotte, stopping to chat under the awnings or inside the shops, his daily routine brought him into constant conversation with Jewish merchants. There were Elias and Cohen, Kahnweiler Brothers, B. Koopman, H. and B. Emanuel, D. Blum, N. Reichenberg, S. Frankenthal, and Asher and Company among the dry goods concerns. The local photographer was a German

Jew named Baumgardener. J. Hirshinger was a pioneer in the manufacture of clothing in the district, and Jonas Schiff established the first local tannery. A branch of the later famous Baruch family also resided in Charlotte during Vance's time. These families almost universally came South with some capital. They helped stabilize conditions after the war by putting this much-needed capital into circulation, by furnishing opportunities for employment, and by opening new fields of endeavor. If the word of older substantial inhabitants is to be taken, these Jews of Reconstruction days were a group of men whose liberality, integrity, and honesty made Jews popular and welcome in Charlotte. The newspapers of the day frequently carried items of Jewish news. Vance's Biblical interests stimulated his study of Jewish history; his firsthand acquaintance with representative Jews and his natural humanitarianism made him plead for tolerance. Together, these strains helped to create the "Scattered Nation."

While Vance's courthouse trials were brightening the gloomy days of Carpetbag government, a new interest presented itself. Vance began to capitalize on his natural speaking ability and to accept professional lecture engagements to supplement his meager income. In the days before the automobile, motion picture, and radio had brought about the "Recreational Revolution," the lyceum was still popular. As early as the campaign of 1860 Vance had been recognized as a stump speaker without peer in the state. During the war inspirational speeches to General Robert E. Lee's army made Vance one of the outstanding orators of the South.[17] Vance's style of speaking was peculiarly his own. His remarkable resourcefulness in adapting himself to every type of audience by means of local illustrations and interests, and his keen, sparkling wit have been attributed to the Norman and Irish blood in his veins. He had an endless flow of stories to nail down important points. These anecdotes were invariably clear and pointed and always illustrative of some larger theme, and he had the rare ability to go on at almost any length without tiring his audiences. Yet when he was through, amidst the vigorous applause, the main points of his speech had been driven home.

As Vance neared forty, matured perhaps by the war and its aftermath, the bumpkin spellbinder became the successful, serious lecturer. There were two distinct strains in his character which have not always been recognized. More than once his most intimate friends made the mistake of believing that while Vance was an incomparable country jury lawyer and stump speaker, he could not make a success of seriousness. Twice he proved them wrong. In the midst of the Civil War the jocose colonel became the grim, efficient war governor. In 1879 his friends feared that he would be a failure in the Senate, that he would amuse the august body, but would win no respect. Again they were mistaken. Like Lincoln, Vance was one of the few men who could successfully combine incessant jocularity with seriousness and get credit for seriousness.

Vance's first important lecture after the war was "The Duties of Defeat" which he delivered as the commencement address at the University of North Carolina, June 7, 1866. He spent much time in careful preparation, and the address was well received. Soon the Tar Heel orator was speaking in large lecture halls in Baltimore, Philadelphia, and New Orleans, to county fairs, historical societies, boards of trade, and graduating classes.[18] He spent his evenings at home and in small-town hotels while on circuit in the careful preparation of these lectures. With the encouragement of friends at Chapel Hill, he widened his intellectual horizon with much reading. By the early 1870's Vance's national reputation as a platform speaker was firmly established. He continued to speak in all parts of the country to a great variety of audiences until interrupted by serious illness five years before his death. Among his best-known lectures were "The Demagogue" and "The Humorous Side of Politics." As the Civil War crystallized into history he put his intimate knowledge of that conflict to good use and delighted the Yankees of a Grand Army of the Republic post in Boston with "The Political and Social South During the War." Another lecture of this type which received considerable notice was "The Last Days of the War in North Carolina," delivered before the Association of the Maryland Line at Baltimore. These speeches were, of course, written from the southern point of view, but were prepared with meticulous care and with a surprising amount of attention paid to historical accuracy. Despite his careful efforts, however, Vance's Civil War lectures have long since been forgotten. His one literary effort destined to survive dealt with the history of "The Scattered Nation." This fact requires considerable additional explanation.

Major Clement Dowd, Vance's law partner, close friend, and official biographer, believed that it was the love of Biblical history which first turned Vance's attention to the Jews.[19] There can be no question that the influence of his mother and his first wife and the strongly Calvinist surroundings in which he lived account for his unusual acquaintance with and devotion to the "Book of Books." The interest long antedated all Jewish acquaintances and connections. The mother, Mrs. Margaret Baird Vance, was a most unusual woman. Although her letters do not reflect a great deal of formal education, she was steeped in the knowledge of the Bible and such secular masters as Shakespeare and Sir Walter Scott. Tradition asserts that Zeb's intimate knowledge of these works began at his mother's knee.[20] The first Mrs. Vance, born Harriet N. Espy, virtually lived in the pages of the "good book." "Hattie" Vance, daughter of a Presbyterian minister, guided her entire life by Calvinist theology. The same "Institutes of the Christian Religion" which caused James Truslow Adams to call the Puritans Jews in spirit influenced Mrs. Vance's religion deeply. Vance lost his mother and wife within a few weeks.

Both women were eulogized by the North Carolina Presbytery as "mothers in Israel." The same pamphlet went on to say that God's "promises to Abraham hold good now to all who share Abraham's faith."[21] Vance himself wrote that Hattie Espy joined her fortunes with his when he was "a wild & obscure young man."[22] She stimulated his interest in the Bible so that he read it for hours at a time.

Vance's mastery of the Old Testament was said to have exceeded that of any other layman in the Bible-reading Old North State. His speeches, writings, and personal correspondence were saturated with Biblical quotations and illustrations. He wrote to the Confederate Secretary of War that had his undisciplined cavalry been sent as one of the ten plagues against Pharaoh, " 'he never would have followed the children of Israel to the Red Sea. No sir, not an inch!' "[23] The war-torn people of North Carolina were to Vance "this suffering and much oppressed Israel."[24] He told Tammany Hall after the war that the northern Democrats were wandering after "Moabitish women."[25] Vance was not yet a member of the church during his Charlotte days, but with Hattie and the boys he regularly attended the First Presbyterian Church. There he listened to the sermons of Dr. Arnold De Welles Miller. That divine was so interested in the "people of the book" that one Sunday a year he invited all Charlotte Hebrews to his church, sat them in the front pews, and devoted his sermon to the Old Testament.[26] Motivations from this source were not lacking to attract Vance's attention to the possibilities of a lecture on the Jewish people.

Besides his devotion to what he would have termed "sacred history," Vance was very much interested in secular history. Here his interests were divided between the intimate details of the great American conflict in which he had participated and ancient history. He was a vice-president of the Southern Historical Society and helped organize a branch of the association in North Carolina. Unlike so many of his contemporaries in historical associations, North and South, his interests and readings were not confined to the story of the thirteen colonies and the wars and battles of the republic. Vance had a broad reading knowledge of, and acquaintance with, classical history which is readily apparent in all his works. The "Scattered Nation" shows the familiarity of its author with Egyptian, Phoenician, and Carthaginian history. He speaks familiarly of the worship of Isis and Osiris, Baal and Astarte. From quotations one concludes that he had read Tacitus and Josephus. He discusses with ease the Hellenistic influence on Jewish thought. His other speeches and writings give similar evidence of wide reading and intimate acquaintance with the broad movements of general history as they were interpreted by the best writers of his time. The "Scattered Nation" reveals that Vance had even encountered the advance guard of the higher Biblical critics. But his general approach, while rationalistic to some extent, is that of the conventional southern fundamentalist.

Vance's Biblical and historical interests account for the part of the "Scattered Nation" interpreting ancient Jewish history as he saw it. The touching plea for tolerance and justice for the Jew came from other sources. We have already considered what part might have been played by intimate Jewish contacts. Outside of these, Vance was broadly humanitarian, kindhearted, and tolerant. His whole personality and character radiated kindness. Formally within the folds of the Presbyterian Church after 1878, he was never in the least narrow-minded or bigoted. Two years after the death of his wife, he fell in love with and married Mrs. Florence Steele Martin of Louisville. Mrs. Martin was a widow of some means and a devout Catholic. Only one acquainted with the southern Protestant attitude toward Catholicism can appreciate the significance of this step and the concern it caused Vance. He wrote to a close friend that his bride-to-be was suited to him in every way except "that she is

She must have also been open minded

a Catholic. Think of it! What *will* my Presbyterian friends say to me? This part of it gives me much concern, but I am . . . still enough of a boy to scorn policy in such a matter, and to listen somewhat to the suggestions of my heart."[27] The marriage proved to be a most happy one. Occasionally there were rumors that Vance was to be converted to his wife's faith and some looked askance at his tolerance, but on the whole he seems to have made an excellent adjustment. The entire episode, in retrospect, is another example of that open-mindedness in his character which inspired the "Scattered Nation."

Jewish writers of these present gloomy days often look back at the nineteenth century as the "halcyon days" of modern Jewish history. While Aryanism, the "streamlined" Teutonic pogrom, and wholesale anti-Semitic propaganda were still far in the future, anti-Jewish feeling was much more than an abstraction in the 1870's. The very writing and repeated delivery of the "Scattered Nation," and the charges that it refutes, give proof that the Jewish situation even in the United States was far from ideal. There were somewhat less than five hundred Jews in North Carolina at the time Vance wrote the speech, a fact that discounts all political motives.[28] North Carolina had long given concern to the defenders of Jewish rights. The Secession Convention of 1861 had continued in the constitution to refuse the right "of holding any office or place of trust or profit in the civil department" to any person "who shall deny . . . the divine authority either of the Old or New Testaments."[29] The 1865 Convention made no change in the situation, but the Constitutional Convention of 1868, apparently without debate, altered the clause so as to admit Jews to public office.[30] Thus, Vance's plea for social equality came almost immediately after the state had belatedly removed the last remaining Jewish civil disqualifications. In the 1870's, especially in the North, the Jewish question took a new form. Following the Federal victory Jews flocked into the country in larger numbers than ever before. The German-Jewish families who had become wealthy with the boom of the 1860's began to feel discrimination in mountain and seashore resorts and were excluded from certain clubs and fraternities. Social ostracism replaced the religious prejudice of the earlier part of the century.[31] A flood of Gentile voices decried the new attitude as out of harmony with American tradition. Vance's voice was but one of many which included William Cullen Bryant, poet; James Parton, eminent biographer; and James K. Hosmer, historian.[32] Vance's apologia may be considered as part of the reaction against the anti-Jewish feeling attendant upon the first large wave of Jewish immigration to these shores. Because of its author's position and eloquence and because of its essential coherence and beauty it was the only part of this type of American Judaica of the period to survive.

The date of the first composition and delivery of the "Scattered Nation" is unknown. The year 1882 has often been incorrectly cited in various oratorical collections which have reprinted the speech. The New York *Tribune* of July 17, 1876, mentions the speech as having been repeatedly delivered by Vance. Internal evidence within the essay would indicate that it was written sometime between 1868 and 1873.[33] It was undoubtedly one of those lectures which Vance delivered during his Charlotte years to supplement his law income. The exact occasion of the first delivery is similarly lost to history.[34] In later years the speech was repeated an almost countless number of times before Gentile and Jewish audiences. A simple reading of the document, however, would indicate that it was originally intended for the Gentile public.[35] During the course of some fifteen to twenty years in which Vance was repeating the speech, he must have made many changes in the text. It was his custom to alter his lecture topics as he repeated them.[36] The present writer is of the opinion that the "Scattered Nation" underwent considerable revision during the early 1880's.

The Russian pogroms of 1881 had focused much attention on the Jewish question, the matter even entering discussion in the halls of Congress. This interest must have resulted in many additional invitations to deliver the lecture. The final version of the speech mentions the "recent barbarities inflicted upon them in Russia," followed by what is doubtless a description of the pogroms which persisted from April to December, 1881.[37] "How sad it is," Vance said, "again to hear that old cry of Jewish sorrow, which we had hoped to hear no more forever!"[38] Inasmuch as the Russian Jews enjoyed a relative degree of security during the reign of Tsar Alexander II from 1855 to 1881, Vance must have been referring to the events of the last year. The fact that the speech was revised and again popularized during this period would explain the common error of setting 1882 as the date of original composition.[39]

The "Scattered Nation" is distinctly one of Vance's serious efforts. There is little in it to indicate that it was written by a man who enjoyed a reputation for drollery. It is another illustration of the deeper, metaphysical side of Zebulon Vance, so often clouded by his delightful wit and easy mannerism. The lecture is a composition resulting from Vance's mastery of the Old Testament and conventional secondary accounts on Jewish subjects. It is written in beautiful imagery and garnished with apt and unusual quotations from literature. The name of the speech is not original.[40] Vance's extra-Biblical sources are often readily discernible. He introduced his subject with a striking description of the Gulf Stream from the famous southern oceanographer, Matthew Fontaine Maury. This was followed by an analogy of Israel to the Gulf Stream—a river of people winding through the sea of nations. He turned to the dawn of Jewish history by quoting at length a condensation of the articles on the subject in the *American Cyclopaedia*.[41] Vance mentioned his indebtedness to *The History of the Jews* by Henry Hart Milman. Dean Milman was a nineteenth-century English clergyman whose attitude toward Jewish history was both rationalistic and sympathetic. For Jewish contributions to medieval civilization, Vance consulted John W. Draper's *History of the Intellectual Development of Europe*. Draper was a contemporary professor of chemistry at New York University whose historical writings were then in vogue. While Vance's researches were far from exhaustive, the essay exhibits a considerable amount of careful preparation. The entire effort is woven into the background of general reading and knowledge. Its chief survival value lies in its beautiful rhetoric, logical organization, and, in parts, originality and freshness.

A detailed analysis of the "Scattered Nation" is beyond the scope of the present article. Even if space permitted, a condensation would be out of order with the majestic original so easily accessible. The timber beams around which the lecture is constructed are: the introduction, the origin of the Jewish people and their religion, the Jewish theocratic state, its condition in Biblical times, the present state of the Jews—their habits and peculiarities, the question of persecution, and the peroration. In places Vance reveals his southern prejudices. For the sake of the Negro, constitutions were violated, laws and partisan courts were used to force an unnatural racial equality, yet Jews, "those from whom we derive our civilization, kinsmen, after the flesh, of Him whom we esteem as the Son of God and Savior of Men, [are] ignomin[i]ously ejected from hotels and watering places as unworthy the association of men who had grown rich by the sale of a new brand of soap or an improved patent rat-trap!"[42] Vance went on to say that he did not question the existence of "Jewish scoundrels in great abundance," but as to the prevalence of Gentile knaves in still greater numbers, "Southern reconstruction put that fact beyond a peradventure."[43] Nor could he miss the opportunity of a thrust at some of his Yankee friends: "Is there any man who hears me to-night," he asked his audiences, "who, if a Yankee and a Jew were to 'lock horns' in a regular encounter of commercial wits, would not give large odds on the Yankee? My own opinion is that the genuine 'guessing' Yankee, with a jackknife and a pine shingle could in two hours time whittle the smartest Jew in New York out of his homestead in the Abrahamic covenant."[44]

Unlike many Judeophiles, Vance did not overstate his case. He did not paint the modern Jews as a people incapable of the foibles of the other species of mankind. Perhaps it was Vance's kindly objectivity that explains the strength of his plea. Despite seventy years of kaleidoscopic events, the "Scattered Nation" is still a vigorous answer to twentieth-century anti-Semitism. "Strike out all of Judaism from the Christian church," he said, "and there remains nothing but an unmeaning superstition."[45] The Jew should be judged "as we judge other men—*by his merits*. And above all, let us cease the abominable injustice of holding the *class* responsible for the sins of the *individual*. We apply this test to no other people."[46]

How many times and in which cities Vance delivered the "Scattered Nation" can only be a matter of surmise. A number of invitations from Jewish and Gentile organizations to speak on the subject are in the Vance Papers, but these are only fragmentary. For instance, in 1878 "The Israelites of Goldsboro" sent Vance a formal petition to deliver his "celebrated lecture," the admission proceeds to be used for the benefit of yellow fever sufferers in the South. The petition also contained the request of various Christian clergymen, the Presbyterian minister adding that the speech would also be appreciated "by those of us who are not of Israel." In 1880 twenty-eight members of a Washington church petitioned Vance to deliver the lecture, the receipts to be used for parish work. Over the course of some fifteen years it was delivered hundreds of times and "in almost every important city in the United States."[47] Vance's lecturing ac-

tivities were halted by the loss of an eye in 1889. This was
a great emotional shock, and he was never quite himself for
the remaining five years of his life. But he had been active
long enough to make a profound and lasting impression on
Christian-Jewish relations in North Carolina. A funeral
oration by a Gentile member of the Charlotte bar reads in
part: "Zeb Vance is dead! The Scattered Nation gathers
round his tomb and weeps. No High Priest, clad in Heaven-
appointed robes, e'er plead the cause of Israel's race more
valiantly than he."[48] The Charlotte *Observer* commented
on a memorial meeting held at the time of Vance's death:
"Perhaps there never was before a memorial meeting held
in honor of a great Gentile prince at which a representative
of the Israelitish nation stood up and paid such a tribute as
did Samuel Wittkowsky yesterday to the memory of Zebulon B. Vance. The scene was unique if not unprecedented
and unparalleled."[49] Nor has the "Scattered Nation" lecture
been forgotten by North Carolinians throughout the years.
It has become a part of southern literature reprinted in
*Oratory of the South, Modern Eloquence, Library of South-
ern Literature*, and in three separate, bound editions.[50] As
late as 1928 a new edition was published by Alfred Wil-
liams and Company of Raleigh, and at present there are
plans under way for still another edition. In 1922 the lecture was reprinted in full in the Asheville *Citizen* at the
request of a non-Jewess.[51] The Greensboro *Daily News*
of January 31, 1926, termed Vance "the latest Jewish
prophet" whose famous lecture "has almost attained a place
in Hebrew sacred literature." The past decade of Jewish
torment has more than once given rise to the vain regret,
"would that the voice of Vance were heard again in the
land."[52]

With the exception of his North Carolina "Israelitish in-
timates," Vance's Jewish connections do not appear to have
been extensive. One finds among his effects an occasional
elaborately engraved tribute from a Jewish congregation

or society. A typical one encloses a "small tribute" for his efforts and concludes: "Believing as we do in the God of Israel, the God of the Bible, the prayers of this portion of the 'Scattered Nation' will be sincerely offered in your behalf."[53] But if an argument from silence is valid, Vance was not on intimate terms with the Jewish leaders of his day. Such Jewish correspondence as is preserved is almost entirely from obscure persons. For instance, a Reverend S. Gerstmann of St. Joseph, Missouri, wanted the Senator's help in 1878 in securing a rabbinical position in Richmond.[54] Six years later the reverend gentleman hinted that with the Democratic return to power, he would not be averse to accepting the Jerusalem consulship.[55] Of great significance is the fact that the American-Jewish press took very little notice of Vance's death. The *Israelite* of Cincinnati and the *American-Hebrew* of New York did not mention his passing. The New York *Jewish Messenger* carried a short notice of the event, adding that the late Senator Vance "had the courage to say on the platform a good word for the Jew, and did his share to teach his countrymen, North and South, some needed lessons in justice and brotherhood."[56]

Adequate Jewish appreciation of Vance's services did not come until after his death. The 1904 and 1916 editions of the essay found their way into many Jewish homes and libraries. Jewish recognition of Vance's memory has grown with the years. Shortly after the close of the World War of 1914–1918, the venerable philanthropist, Nathan Strauss, went to Asheville, laid a wreath on Vance's monument, and said that he did not want to die without discharging a debt of gratitude.[57] It was Strauss, too, who built a suitable fence around the monument in Asheville City Square. In 1928 the Asheville Lodge of B'nai Brith dedicated a plaque to Vance's memory in the yard of Old Calvary Church at Asheville, in a place which has been called the "Westminster Abbey of the Southland." An assemblage of several thousand, including many dignitaries, were present that crisp fall day when Rabbi Stephen S. Wise formally expressed the tribute of American Jewry to Vance.[58]

The dark years of the 1930's have brought the members of the "Scattered Nation" even closer to Vance's memory. The *American-Jewish Times* of September, 1936, reprinted the famous lecture in full in its New Year's edition as a message of hope and consolation to the Jews of the world. The sparks of European racial hatred and intolerance have even fallen in the very shadow of Vance's birthplace. With them has come a refreshing counteraction from the font of his memory. Each May 13, Vance's birthday, the Asheville representatives of the United Daughters of the Confederacy and B'nai Brith sponsor a program around the Vance monument. Here, in the presence of the city officials and representatives of other organizations, due tribute is paid to the memory of this beloved North Carolinian. Despite intensive devotion to his native state and section, Zebulon B. Vance was first of all a great American. The paramount lesson of his essay is that the people of the United States allow the prejudices engendered by two thousand years of Old World history to wither in the fresher breezes of the New World atmosphere.

Reprinted from *The Journal of Southern History*, Vol. VII, No. 3, August, 1941.

SELIG ADLER

1909–1985

Selig Adler was born in Baltimore on January 22, 1909. He received his bachelor of arts degree from the University of Buffalo in 1931, his masters and doctorate degrees from the University of Illinois in 1932 and 1934. He was a Distinguished Professor of History at the University of Buffalo (later the State University of New York at Buffalo). He served as Visiting Professor of History at Cornell University in 1951 and 1959, and as Visiting Professor of History at the University of Rochester in 1952 and 1953. He was the author of *The Isolationist Impulse 1957*, *From Ararat to Suburbia 1960*, and *The Uncertain Giant 1965*.

NOTES TO CHAPTER TWO

1. Charlotte *Observer*, April 19, 1894.
2. R. D. W. Connor, *Makers of North Carolina History* (Raleigh, 1911), 239.
3. *The Ceremonies Attending the Unveiling of the Bronze Statue of Zeb B. Vance, LL.D. in Capitol Square, Raleigh, N. C., and the Address of Richard H. Battle, LL.D., August 22, 1900* (Raleigh, 1900), 38.
4. Statement of Isidore Wallace, Statesville, North Carolina, to the writer, July 27, 1939.
5. Statement of Noble Bloomfield Mills to the writer, July 27, 1939. Mr. Mills had lived all his eighty-seven years in Statesville or the immediate vicinity, and in 1939 was still actively engaged in business.
6. Statement of Isidore Wallace to the writer, July 27, 1939.
7. Samuel Wittkowsky to Zebulon B. Vance, January 29, 1865, in Zebulon B. Vance Papers (North Carolina Historical Commission, Raleigh); Clement Dowd, *Life of Zebulon B. Vance* (Charlotte, 1897), 95. The writer wishes to express his thanks to Dr. Charles C. Crittenden, secretary of the Commission, and to other members of the staff who allowed him to make use of the material, and who with patience and helpful suggestions guided his way through the many volumes of Vance material.
8. Unidentified newspaper clipping found among a collection of Vance Clippings in the North Carolina Room, University of North Carolina Library. A slightly different version of Vance's conversation with Wittkowsky may be found in Dowd, *Zebulon B. Vance*, 96.
9. Dowd, *Zebulon B. Vance*, 352.
10. Phillips Russell, "Hooraw for Vance!" in *American Mercury* (New York, 1924–), XXII (1931), 238.
11. John B. Alexander, *The History of Mecklenburg County from 1740 to 1900* (Charlotte, 1902), 379.
12. Daniel A. Tompkins, *History of Mecklenburg Co. and the City of Charlotte from 1740 to 1903*, 2 vols. (Charlotte, 1904), I, 140.
13. Alexander, *History of Mecklenburg County*, 335 ff.
14. Unidentified newspaper clipping from a collection in the possession of the Mechanics Perpetual Building and Loan Association, Charlotte, North Carolina.
15. *Ibid.*
16. Unidentified newspaper clipping, in Vance Clippings.
17. Connor, *Makers of North Carolina History*, 233–234.

18. Dowd, *Zebulon B. Vance*, 220.

19. *Ibid.*, 121.

20. Greensboro *Daily News*, January 31, 1926.

21. *In Memory of Mrs. Margaret M. Vance and Mrs. Hariette Espy Vance* (Raleigh, 1878), 8, 25.

22. Vance to Cornelia P. Spencer, December 10, 1878, in Cornelia P. Spencer Papers (North Carolina Historical Commission, Raleigh).

23. Quoted in Russell, "Hooraw for Vance!" in *loc. cit.*, 233.

24. Vance to David L. Swain, September 22, 1864, quoted in unidentified newspaper clipping in Vance Papers.

25. Vance made this statement in his Tammany Hall speech of July 4, 1886. D. W. McCauley to Vance, July 19, 1886, *ibid.*

26. Statement of Frank D. Alexander, Charlotte, to the writer, July 27, 1939.

27. Vance to Spencer, May 6, 1880, in Spencer Papers.

28. Iser L. Freund, "Brief History of the Jews of North Carolina" (MS. in possession of the University of North Carolina Library).

29. Leon Huhner, "The Struggle for Religious Liberty in North Carolina, with Special Reference to the Jews," in American Jewish Historical Society, *Publications* (Baltimore, 1893–), No. 16 (1907), 37–71; Francis N. Thorpe (ed.), *The Federal and State Constitutions, Colonial Charters, and Other Organic Laws of the . . . United States of America*, 7 vols. (Washington, 1909), V, 2793.

30. Huhner, "The Struggle for Religious Liberty in North Carolina," in *loc. cit.*, 68.

31. Alice H. Rhine, "Race Prejudice at Summer Resorts," in *Forum* (New York, 1886–), III (1887), 523–531.

32. *Ibid.*, 524, 529; James Parton, "Our Israelitish Brethren," in *Atlantic Monthly* (Boston, 1857–), XXVI (1870), 385–403.

33. The earliest reference that the writer has been able to find concerning the "Scattered Nation" was written in 1875. By that date it seems that the lecture was already well known. The speech begins, "Says Professor Maury." Matthew Fontaine Maury did not enter academic life until 1868 when he became a member of the faculty of the Virginia Military Institute, so the introduction was written after 1868. Maury died in 1873, yet there is no mention of the "late distinguished Professor," or some other tribute that Vance would have likely paid a recently deceased eminent ex-Confederate. The introduction, then, sounds very much as if it were written before Maury's death. There is other circumstantial evidence which would warrant putting the date of composition between the above-mentioned years. See H. A. Marmer, "Matthew Fontaine Maury," in *Dictionary of American Biography*, 20 vols. and index (New York, 1928–1937), XII, 430–431.

34. Tradition asserts that the "Scattered Nation" was first delivered in Baltimore. The writer was unable to find any corroboration after a search which included visits to the Peabody Institute and Enoch Pratt Free libraries in Baltimore. Yet, in view of Vance's close Baltimore connections, especially in the person of Dr. Thomas J. Boykin, the former surgeon of his regiment, the tradition may well be founded in fact.

35. For instance, Vance's statement that the Jews "trouble neither you nor me." Dowd, *Zebulon B. Vance*, 388. All quotations and refer-

ences to the "Scattered Nation" are to the version in *ibid.*, 369–399. The various editions of the speech differ in minor details.

36. In an undated letter to an unidentified correspondent, in the Vance Papers, Vance wrote: "No danger of my publishing my Lecture. I want to repeat it, and I agree with you that it is not prudent to put it in print. I have rewritten it, and 'woven in the thread' you mention." This reference may or may not be to the "Scattered Nation."

37. Herman Rosenthal, "Alexander III., Alexandrovich," in *Jewish Encyclopedia*, 12 vols. (New York, 1901–1906), I, 347. Vance also spoke of the new German anti-Semitism. It is hardly probable that he had heard of this new movement until after 1878, for it was then that Bismarck turned to the program of the reactionaries. This part of the speech also was probably added in 1882. Gotthard Deutsch, "Anti-Semitism," *ibid.*, 644–645.

38. Dowd, *Zebulon B. Vance*, 394.

39. Ashley H. Thorndike (ed.), *Modern Eloquence*, 15 vols. (New York, 1936), XIII, 396. This source states that the speech was "delivered in 1882 and thereafter in various places." The same date is given in various other oratorical and literary collections.

40. For instance, *The Scattered Nation; Past, Present and Future*, a missionary periodical addressed to the Jews, was published in London in the 1860's. The *Israelite* of March 3, 1871, a Cincinnati Jewish organ, published an article under the same title. It is hardly possible that the author of this article had ever heard of Vance's lecture at this early date, if indeed Vance had already written it.

41. "Hebrews," in *American Cyclopaedia*, 16 vols. (New York, 1873–1876), VIII, 582 ff.

42. Dowd, *Zebulon B. Vance*, 393.

43. *Ibid.*, 396.

44. *Ibid.*, 397.

45. *Ibid.*, 374.

46. *Ibid.*, 393.

47. R. D. W. Connor, "Zebulon Baird Vance," in *Dictionary of American Biography*, XIX, 161.

48. Edwin D. Shurter (ed.), *Oratory of the South, From the Civil War to the Present Time* (New York, 1908), 181. This eulogy by Charles W. Tillett has been reprinted in many places. If often appears without the paragraph concerning the "Scattered Nation." It is possible that this section was added later, although the rest of the eulogy was written at the time of Vance's death. Dowd, *Zebulon B. Vance*, 327–329, reprinted Tillett's eulogy in 1897 without this paragraph.

49. Charlotte *Observer*, April 17, 1894.

50. The speech was printed, probably in the newspapers, at least as early as 1878. A petition for its delivery in Goldsboro, dated 1878, and found in the Vance Papers, mentions that many of the petitioners had already read the speech. Dowd, *Zebulon B. Vance*, 369–399, reprinted it in full in 1897. The first separately bound edition was published privately by Willis Bruce Dowd in 1904 and contained an introduction by the publisher. The 1916 edition was printed in New York with the 1904 introduction and a foreword by M. Schnitzer. The 1928 edition was published in Raleigh and has an introduction by Rabbi

Moses P. Jacobson, then of Asheville. It was sponsored by the Asheville Lodge of B'nai Brith in connection with the unveiling of the Vance plaque in that city. At the present writing, District Grand Lodge Number Five, B'nai Brith, is contemplating a fourth edition.

51. Asheville *Citizen*, February 8, 1922.

52. *Ibid.*, May 13, 1938.

53. Tribute to Vance from an unidentified Jewish social organization, in Vance Papers.

54. S. Gerstmann to Vance, August 7, 1878, *ibid.*

55. *Id.* to *id.*, November 30, 1884, *ibid.*

56. New York *Jewish Messenger*, April 27, 1894.

57. Statement of D. Hiden Ramsey, general manager and secretary of the Asheville Citizen-Times Company, Asheville, N. C., to the writer, July 28, 1939.

58. Raleigh *News and Observer*, October 15, 1928; Asheville *Citizen*, October 14, 15, 1928.

"The Scattered Nation"

CHAPTER THREE

"The Scattered Nation"

BY ZEBULON B. VANCE

Says Prof. Maury: "There is a river in the ocean. In the severest droughts it never fails, and in the mightiest floods it never overflows. The Gulf of Mexico is its fountain, and its mouth is in the Arctic seas. It is the Gulf Stream. There is in the world no other such majestic flow of waters. Its current is more rapid than the Mississippi or the Amazon, and its volume more than a thousand times greater. Its waters, as far out from the Gulf as the Carolina coasts, are of an indigo blue; they are so distinctly marked that their line of junction with the common sea-water may be traced by the eye. Often one-half of a vessel may be perceived floating in Gulf stream water, while the other half is in common water of the sea, so sharp is the line and such the want of affinity between those waters, and such too the reluctance, so to speak, on the part of those of the Gulf Stream to mingle with the common water of the sea."

This curious phenomenon in the physical world has its counterpart in the moral. There is a lonely river in the midst of the ocean of mankind. The mightiest floods of human temptation have never caused it to overflow and the fiercest fires of human cruelty, though seven times heated in the furnace of religious bigotry, have never caused it to dry up, although its waves for two thousand years have rolled crimson with the blood of its martyrs. Its fountain is in the grey dawn of the world's history, and its mouth is somewhere in the shadows of eternity. It too refuses to mingle with the surrounding waves, and the line which divides its restless billows from the common waters of humanity is also plainly visible to the eye. It is the Jewish race.

The Jew is beyond doubt the most remarkable man of this world—past or present. Of all the stories of the sons of men, there is none so wild, so wonderful, so full of extreme mutation, so replete with suffering and horror, so abounding in extraordinary providences, so overflowing with scenic romance. There is no man who approaches him in the extent and character of the influence which he has exercised over the human family. His history is the history of our civilization and progress in this world, and our faith and hope in that which is to come. From him have we derived the form and pattern of all that is excellent on earth or in heaven. If, as DeQuincey says, the Roman Emperors, as the great accountants for the happiness of more men and men more cultivated than ever before, were entrusted to the motions of a single will, had a special, singular and mysterious relation to the secret councils of heaven—thrice truly may it be said of the Jew. Palestine, his home, was the central chamber of God's administration. He was at once the grand usher to these glorious courts, the repository of the councils of the Almighty and the envoy of the divine mandates to the consciences of men. He was the priest and faith-giver to mankind, and as such, in spite of the jibe and jeer, he must ever be considered as occupying a peculiar and sacred relation to all other peoples of this world. Even now, though the Jews have long since ceased to exist as a consolidated nation, inhabiting a common country, and for eighteen hundred years have been scattered far and near over the wide earth, their strange customs, their distinct features, personal peculiarities and their *scattered unity*, make them still a wonder and an astonishment.

Though dead as a nation—as we speak of nations—they yet live. Their ideas fill the world and move the wheels of its progress, even as the sun, when he sinks behind the Western hills, yet fills the heavens with the remnants of his glory. As the destruction of matter in one form is made necessary to its resurrection in another, so it would seem that the perishing of the Jewish nationality was in order to the universal acceptance and the everlasting establishment of Jewish ideas. Never before was there an instance of such a general rejection of the person and character, and acceptance of the doctrines and dogmas of a people.

We admire with unlimited admiration the Greek and Roman, but reject with contempt his crude and beastly divinities. We affect to despise the Jew, but accept and adore the pure conception of a God which he taught us, and whose real existence the history of the Jew more than all else establishes. When the Court Chaplain of Frederick the Great was asked by that bluff monarch for a brief and concise summary of the argument in support of the truths of Scripture, he instantly replied, with a force to which nothing could be added, "The Jews, Your Majesty, the Jews."

I propose briefly to glance at their history, origin and civilization, peculiarities, present condition and probable destiny.

"A people of Semitic race," says the Encyclopaedia, "whose ancestors appear at the very dawn of the history of mankind, on the banks of Euphrates, the Jordan and the Nile, their fragments are now to be seen in larger or smaller numbers, in almost all of the cities of the globe, from Batavia to New Orleans, from Stockholm to Cape Town. When little more numerous than a family, they had their language, customs and peculiar observances, treated with princes and in every respect acted as a nation. Though broken, as if into atoms, and scattered through all climes, among the rudest and the most civilized nations, they have preserved, through thousands of years, common features and observances, a common religion, literature and sacred language. Without any political union, without any common head or centre, they are generally regarded and regard themselves as a nation. They began as nomads, emigrating from country to country; their law made them agriculturists for fifteen centuries; their exile transformed them into a mercantile people. They have struggled for their national existence against the Egyptians, Assyrians, Babylonians, Syrians and Romans; have been conquered and nearly exterminated by each of these powers and have survived them all. They have been oppressed and persecuted by Emperors and Republics, by Sultans and by Popes, Moors and Inquisitors; they were proscribed in Catholic Spain, Protestant Norway and Greek Muscovy, while their persecutors sang the hymns of their psalmody, revered their books, believed in their prophets and even persecuted them in the name of their God. They have numbered philosophers among the Greeks of Alexandria, and the Saracens of Cordova; have transplanted the wisdom of the East beyond the Pyrenees and the Rhine, and have been treated as pariahs among Pagans, Mohammedans and Christians. They have fought for liberty under Kosciusko and Blucher, and popular assemblies among the Sclavi and Germans, still withheld from them the right of living in certain towns, villages and streets."

Whilst no people can claim such an unmixed purity of blood, certainly none can establish such antiquity of origin, such unbroken generations of descent. That splendid passage of Macaulay so often quoted, in reference to the Roman Pontiffs, loses its force in sight of Hebrew history. "No other institution," says he, "is left standing which carries the mind back to the times when the smoke of sacrifice rose from the Pantheon, and when camels, leopards, and tigers bounded in the Iberian amphitheatre. The proudest royal houses are but of yesterday as compared with the line of the Supreme Pontiffs; that line we trace back in unbroken lines, from the Pope who crowned Napoleon in the nineteenth century, to the Pope who crowned Pepin in the eighth, and far beyond Pepin, the august dynasty extends until it is lost in the twilight of fable. The Republic of Venice came next in antiquity, but the Republic of Venice is modern compared with the Papacy, and the Republic of Venice is gone and the Papacy remains. The Catholic Church was great and respected before the Saxon had set foot on Britain, before the Frank had passed the Rhine, when Grecian eloquence still flourished at Antioch, when idols were still worshipped in the Temple at Mecca; and she may still exist, in undiminished vigor when some traveller from New Zealand in the midst of a vast solitude shall take his stand on a broken arch of London Bridge to sketch the ruins of St. Paul." This is justly esteemed one of the most eloquent passages in our literature, but I submit it is not history.

The Jewish people, church and institutions are still left standing, though the stones of the temple remain no longer one upon the other, though its sacrificial fires are forever extinguished; and though the tribes, whose glory it was, wander with weary feet throughout the earth. And what is the line of Roman Pontiffs compared to that splendid dynasty of the successors of Aaron and Levi? "The twilight of fable," in which the line of Pontiffs began, was but the noonday brightness of the Jewish priesthood. Their institution carries the mind back to the age when the prophet, in rapt mood, stood over Babylon and uttered God's wrath against that grand and wondrous mistress of the Euphratean plains—when the Memphian chivalry still gave precedence to the chariots and horsemen who each morning poured forth from the brazen gates of the abode of Ammon; when Tyre and Sidon were yet building their palaces by the sea, and Carthage, their greatest daughter, was yet unborn. That dynasty of prophetic priest existed even before Clio's pen had learned to record the deeds of men; and when that splendid, entombed civilization once lighted the shores of the Erythræan Sea, the banks of the Euphrates and the plains of Shinar, with a glory inconceivable, of which there is nought now to tell, except the dumb eloquence of ruined temples and buried cities.

Then, too, it must be remembered that these Pontiffs were but Gentiles in the garb of Jews, imitating their whole routine. All Christian churches are but off-shoots from or grafts upon the old Jewish stock. Strike out all of Judaism from the Christian church and there remains nothing but an unmeaning superstition.

The Christian is simply the successor of the Jew—the glory of the one is likewise the glory of the other. The Saviour of the world was, after the flesh, a Jew—born of a Jewish maiden; so likewise were all of the apostles and first propagators of Christianity. The Christian religion is equally Jewish with that of Moses and the prophets.

I am not unaware of the fact that other people besides the Semites had a conception of the true God long before He was revealed to Abraham. The Hebrew Scriptures themselves testify this, and so likewise do the books of the very oldest of written records. The fathers of the great Aryan race, the shepherds of Iran had so vivid a conception of the unity of God, as to give rise to the opinion that they too had once had a direct revelation. It is more likely, however, that traditions of this God had descended among them from the Deluge which ultimately became adulterated by polytheistic imaginings. It seems natural that these people of highly sensitive intellects, dwelling beneath the serene skies, that impend over the plains and mountains of Southwestern Asia, thickly studded with the calm and glorious stars, should mistake these most majestic emblems of the Creator for the Creator himself. Hence no doubt, arose the worship of light and fire by the Iranians, and Sabæanism or star worship by the Chaldeans. But the better opinion of learned orientalists is that while the outward or exoteric doctrine taught the worship of the symbols, the esoteric or secret doctrines of Zoroaster, his predecessors and disciples, taught in fact the worship of the *Principle, the First Cause, the Great Unknown, the Universal Intelligence, Magdam or God*. There can be no doubt that Abraham brought this monotheistic conception with him from Chaldea; but notwithstanding this dim traditional light, which was abroad outside of the race of Shem, perhaps over the entire breadth of that splendid prehistoric civilization of the Arabian Cushite, yet for the more perfect light, which revealed to us God and His attributes, we are unquestionably indebted to the Jew.

We owe to him, if not the conception, at least the preservation of pure monotheism. For whether this knowledge was original with these eastern people or traditional merely, it was speedily lost, by all of them except the Jews. Whilst an unintelligent use of symbolism enveloped the central figure with a cloud of idolatry and led the Magi to the worship of Light and Fire, the Sabaean to the adoration of the heavenly host, the Egyptian to bowing down before Isis and Osiris, the Carthaginian to the propitiation of Baal and Astarte by human sacrifice and the subtle Greek to the deification of the varied laws of Nature; the bearded Prophets of Israel were ever thundering forth, "Know O Israel, that the Lord thy God is one God, and Him only shalt thou serve."

Even his half-brother Ishmael, after an idolatrous sleep of centuries, awoke with a sharp and bloody protest against Polytheism, and established the unity of God as the cornerstone of his faith. In this respect the influence which the Jew has exercised over the destinies of mankind place him before all the men of this world. For in this idea of God, all of the faith and creeds of the dominant peoples of the earth centre. It divides like a great mountain range the civilizations of the ancient and modern worlds. Many enlightened men of antiquity acknowledged the beauty of this conception, though they did not embrace it. Socrates did homage to it, and Josephus declares that he derived his sublime ideal from the Jewish Scriptures. The accomplished Tacitus seemed to grasp it, as the following passage will show. In speaking of the Jews and in contrasting them with the Egyptians, he says: "With regard to the Deity, their creed is different. The Egyptians worship various animals and also certain symbolical representatives which are the work of man. The Jews acknowledge one God only, and Him they see in the mind's eye, and Him they adore in contemplation, condemning as impious idolaters, all who with perishable materials wrought into the human form, attempt to give a representation of the Deity. The God of the Jews is the great governing mind that directs and guides the whole frame of nature—eternal, infinite and neither capable of change or subject to decay."

This matchless and eloquent definition of the Deity has never been improved upon, but it seems that it made slight impression upon the philosophical historian's mind. And yet what a contrast it is with his own coarse, material gods! Indeed the rejection or ignorance of this pure conception by the acute and refined intellects of the mediæval ancients strikes us with wonder, and illustrates the truth, that no man by searching can find out God. I am not unaware that the Arabian idea of Deity received many modifications from the conceptions of adjoining and contemporary nations— by cross-fertilization of ideas, as the process has been called. From the Egyptians and Assyrians were received many of these modifications, but the chief impression was from the Greeks. The general effect was to broaden and enlarge the original idea, whose tendency was to regard the Supreme Being as a *tribal* Deity, into the grander, universal God, or Father of all. If time permitted it would be a most interesting study to trace the action and reaction of Semitic upon Hellenistic thought. How Hellenistic philosophy produced Pharisaism or the progressive party of the Hebrew Theists;

how Pharisaism in turn produced Stoicism, which again prepared the way for Christianity itself.

The whole polity of the Jews was originally favorable to agriculture; and though they adhered to it closely for many centuries, yet, the peculiar facilities of their country ultimately forced them largely into commerce. The great caravan routes from the rich countries of the East, Mesopotamia, Shinar, Babylonia, Media, Assyria and Persia, to the ports of the Mediterranean, lay through Palestine, whilst Spain, Italy, Gaul, Asia Minor, Northern Africa, Egypt, and all the riches that then clustered around the shores of the Great Sea and upon the islands in its bosom, had easy access to its harbors. In fact the wealth of the world, its civilization, refinement and art lay in concentric circles around Jerusalem as a focal point. The Jewish people grew rich in spite of themselves and gradually forsook their agricultural simplicity.

But more than all things else their institutions interest mankind. Their laws for the protection of property, the enforcement of industry and the upholding of the state were such as afforded the strongest impulse to personal freedom and national vigor. The great principle of their real estate laws was the inalienability of the land. Houses in walled towns might be sold in perpetuity, if unredeemed within the year; land only for a limited period. At the year of Jubilee every estate reverted without repurchase to the original owners, and even during this period it might be redeemed by paying the value of the purchase of the year which intervened until the Jubilee. Little as we may now be disposed to value this remarkable Agrarian law, says Dean Milman, it secured the political equality of the people and anticipated all the mischiefs so fatal to the early Republics of Greece and Italy, the appropriation of the whole territory of the State, by a rich and powerful landed oligarchy, with the consequent convulsing of the community from the deadly struggles between the patrician and the plebeian orders. In the Hebrew state the improvident man might indeed reduce himself and his family to penury or servitude, but he could not perpetuate a race of slaves or paupers. Every fifty years God the King and Lord of the soil, as it were, resumed the whole territory and granted it back in the same portions to the descendants of the original possessors.

It is curious to observe, continues the same author, in this earliest practicable Utopia, the realization of Machiavelli's great maxim, the constant renovation of a state, according to the first principles of its constitution, a maxim recognized by our own statesmen, which they designate as a "frequent recurrence to the first principles." How little we learn that is new. The civil polity of the Jews is so intimately blended historically with the ecclesiastical that the former is not easily comprehended by the ordinary student. Their scriptures relate principally to the latter, and to obtain a knowledge of the other, resort must be had to the Talmud and the Rabbinical expositions, a task that few men will let themselves to, who hope to do anything else in this world. Yet a little study will repay richly the political student, by showing him the origin of many excellent seminal principles which we regard as modern. Their government was in form a theocratic democracy. God was not only their spiritual but their temporal sovereign also, who promulgated his laws by the mouths of his inspired prophets. Hence their terrible and unflagging denunciations of all forms of idolatry—it was not only a sin against pure religion, but it was treason also. In most other particulars theirs was a democracy far purer than that of Athens. The very important principle of the separation of the functions of government was recognized. The civil and ecclesiastical departments were kept apart, the civil ruler exercised no ecclesiastic functions and vice versa. When, as sometimes happened, the two functions rested in the same man, they were yet exercised differently, as was not long since our custom in the administration of equity as contra-distinguished from law.

Their organic law containing the elements of their polity, though given by God Himself, was yet required to be solemnly ratified by the whole people. This was done on Ebal and Gerizim and is perhaps the first, as it is certainly the grandest constitutional convention ever held among men. On these two lofty mountains, separated by a deep and narrow ravine, all Israel, comprising three millions of souls, were assembled; elders, prophets, priests, women and children, and 600,000 warriors, led by the spears of Judah and supported by the archers of Benjamin. In this mighty presence, surrounded by the sublime accessions to the grandeur of the scene, the law was read by the Levites line by line, item by item, whilst the tribes on either height signified their acceptance thereof by responsive amens, which pierced the heavens. Of all the great principles established for the happiness and good government of our race, though hallowed by the blood of the bravest and the best, and approved by centuries of trial, no one had a grander origin, or a more glorious exemplification than this one, that all governments derive their just powers from the consent of the governed.

So much for their organic law. Their legislation upon the daily exigencies and development of their society was also provided for on the most radically democratic basis, with the practical element of representation. The Sanhedrin legislated for all ecclesiastical affairs, and had also original judicial powers and jurisdiction over all offenses against the religious law, and appellate jurisdiction of many other offenses. It was the principal body of their polity, as religion was the principal object of their constitution. It was thoroughly representative. Local and municipal government was fully recognized. The legislation for a city was done by the elders thereof, the prototypes in name and character of our eldermen or aldermen.

They were the keystone of the whole social fabric, and so directly represented the people, that the terms "elders" and "people" are often used as synonymous. The legislation for a tribe was done by the princes of that tribe, and the heads of families thereof; whilst the elders of all the cities, heads of all the families and princes of all the tribes when assembled, constituted the National Legislature, or congregation. The functions of this representative body, however, were gradually usurped and absorbed by the Sanhedrin.

So thoroughly recognized was the principle of representation that no man exercised any political rights in his individual capacity, but only as a member of the house, which was the basis of the Hebrew polity. The ascending scale was the family or collection of houses, the tribe or collection of families and the congregation or collection of tribes.

The Kingdom thus composed was in fact a confederation, and exemplified both its strength and its weakness. The tribes were equal and sovereign within the sphere of their individual concerns. A tribe could convene its own legislative body at pleasure; so could any number of tribes convene a joint body whose enactments were binding only upon the tribes represented therein. A single tribe or any number combined could make treaties, form alliances and wage war, whilst the others remained at peace with the enemy of their brethren. They were to all intents and purposes independent States, joined together for common objects on the principle of federal republics, with a general government of delegated and limited powers. Within their tribal boundaries their sovereignty was absolute minus only the powers granted to the central agent. They elected their chiefs, generals and kings. Next to the imperative necessity of common defense their bond of union was their divine constitution, one religion and one blood. Justice was made simple and was administered cheaply. Among no people in this world did the law so recognize the dignity and sacred nature of man made in the image of God and the creature of his especial covenanting care.

The constitution of their criminal courts and their code of criminal laws was most remarkable. The researches of the learned have failed to discover in all antiquity anything so explicit, so humane, and embracing so many of what are now considered the essential elements of enlightened jurisprudence. Only four offenses were punished by death. By English law, no longer ago than the reign of George I, more than 150 offenses were so punishable! The court for the trial of these capital offenders was the local Sanhedrin, composed of twenty-three members, who were both judges and jurors, prosecuting attorneys and counsel for the accused.

The tests applied both to them, and the accusing witnesses, as to capacity and impartiality, were more rigid than those known to exist anywhere else in the world. The whole procedure was so guarded as to convey the idea that the first object was to save the criminal.

From the first step of the accusation to the last moment preceding final execution, no caution was neglected, no solemnity was omitted, that might aid the prisoner's acquittal. No man in any way interested in the result, no gamester of any kind, no usurer, no store dealer, no relative of accused or accuser, no seducer or adulterer, no man without a fixed trade or business, could sit on that court. Nor could any aged man whose infirmities might make him harsh, nor any childless man or bastard, as being insensible to the relations of parent and child.

Throughout the whole system of the Jewish government there ran a broad, genuine and refreshing stream of democracy, such as the world then knew little of, and has since but little improved. For of course the political student will not be deceived by names. It matters not what their chief magistrates and legislators were called, if in fact and in substance, their forms were eminently democratic. Masters of political philosophy tell us—and tell us with truth—that power in a State must and will reside with those who own the soil. If the land belongs to a king the government is a despotism, though every man in it voted; if the land belongs to a select few, it is an aristocracy: but if it belongs to the many, it is a democracy, for here is the division of power. Now, where, either in the ancient or modern world, will you find such a democracy as that of Israel? For where was there ever such a perfect and continuing division of the land among the people? It was impossible for this power ever to be concentrated in the hands of one or a select few. The lands belonged to God as the head of the Jewish nation —the right of eminent domain, so to speak, was in Him— and the people were His tenants.

The year of Jubilee, as we have seen, came ever in time to blast the schemes of the ambitious and designing.

Their law provided for no standing army, the common defense was entrusted to the patriotism of the people, who kept and bore arms at will, and believing that their hills and valleys would be best defended by footmen, the use of cavalry was forbidden, lest it should tend to feed the passion for foreign conquest.

The ecclesiastical Sanhedrin as before observed, was the principal body of their polity. Its members were composed of the wisest and most learned of their people, who expounded and enforced the law and supervised all the inferior courts. This exposition upon actual cases arising did not suffice the learned doctors, who made the great mistake which modern courts have learned to avoid, of uttering their *dicta* in anticipated cases. These decisions and dicta constitute the ground work of the Talmuds, of which there are two copies extant. They constitute the most remarkable collection of oriental wisdom, abstruse learning, piety, blasphemy and obscenity ever got together in the world; and bear the same relation to the Jewish law, which our judicial decisions do to our statute law. Could they be disentombed from the mass of rubbish by which they are covered—said to be so great as to deter all students who are not willing to devote a life-time to the task, from entering upon their study—they would no doubt be of inestimable value to theologians, by furnishing all the aids which contemporaneous construction must ever impart.

Time would not permit me if I had the power, to describe the chief city of the Jews, their religious and political capital—"Jerusalem the Holy"—"the dwelling of peace." In the days of Jewish prosperity it was in all things a fair type of this strange country and people. Enthroned upon the hills of Judah, overflowing with riches, the free-will offerings of a devoted people—decked with the barbaric splendor of eastern taste, it was the rival in power and wondrous beauty of the most magnificent cities of antiquity. Nearly every one of her great competitors has mouldered into dust. The bat and the owl inhabit their towers, and the fox litters her young in the corridors of their palaces, but Jerusalem still sits in solitary grandeur upon the lovely hills, and though faded, feeble and ruinous still towers in *moral* splendor above all the spires and domes and pinnacles ever erected by human hands. Nor can I dwell, tempting as is the theme, upon the scenery, the glowing landscapes, the cultivated fields, gardens and vineyards and gurgling fountains of that pleasant land. Many high summits and even one of the towers in the walls of the city of Jerusalem were said to have afforded a perfect view of the whole land from border to border. I must be content with asking you to imagine what a divine prospect would burst upon the vision from the summit of that stately tower; and picture the burning sands of the desert far beyond the mysterious waters of the Dead Sea on the one hand, and the shining waves of the great sea on the other, flecked with the white sails of the Tyrian ships, whilst hoary Lebanon, crowned with its diadem of perpetual snow glittered in the morning light like a dome of fire tempered with the emerald of its cedar—a fillet of glory around its brow. The beauty of that band of God's people, the charm of their songs, the comeliness of their maidens, the celestial peace of their homes, the romance of their national history, and the sublimity of their faith, so entice me, that I would not know when to cease, should I once enter upon their story. I must leave behind, too, the blood-stained record of their last great siege, illustrated by their splendid but unavailing courage; their fatal dissensions and final destruction, with all its incredible horrors; of their exile and slavery, of their dispersion in all lands and kingdoms, of their persecutions, sufferings, wanderings and despair, for eighteen hundred years. Indeed, it is a story that puts to shame not only our Christianity, but our common humanity. It staggers belief to be told, not only that such things could be done at all, by blinded heathen or ferocious Pagan, but done by Christian people and in the name of Him, the meek and lowly, who was called the Prince of Peace, and the harbinger of good will to men. Still it is an instructive story; it seems to mark in colors never to be forgotten, both the wickedness and the folly of intolerance. Truly, it serves to show that the wrath of a religious bigot is more fearful and ingenious than the cruelest of tortures hatched in the councils of hell. It is not my purpose to comment upon the religion of the Jews, nor shall I undertake to say that they gave no cause in the earlier ages of Christianity for the hatred of their opponents. Undoubtedly they gave much cause, and exhibited themselves much bitterness and ferocity towards the followers of the Nazarene; which however, it may be an excuse, is far from being a justification of the centuries of horror which followed. But if constancy, faithfulness and devotion to principle under the most trying circumstances to which the children of men were ever subjected, be considered virtues, then indeed are the Jews to be admired. They may safely defy the rest of mankind to show such undying ad-

herence to accepted faith, such wholesale sacrifice for con-
science sake. For it they have in all ages given up home and
country, wives and children, gold and goods, ease and shelter and life; for it they endured all the evils of an infernal
wrath for eighteen centuries; for it they have endured, and
—say what you will—endured with an inexpressible manhood that which no other portion of the human family ever
have, or, in my opinion, ever would have endured. For sixty
generations the heritage which the father left the son was
misery, suffering, shame and despair; and that son preserved and handed down to his son, that black heritage as
a golden heir-loom, *for the sake of God.*

A few remarks upon their numbers and present status
in the world, their peculiarities and probable destiny and
my task will be done.

Originally, as we have seen, the Jews were an agricultural people, and their civil polity was framed specially for
this state of things. Indeed the race of Shem originally
seemed not to have been endowed with the great commercial instincts which characterize the descendants of Ham
and Japheth. Their cities for the most part, were built in
the interior, remote from the channels of trade, whilst the
race of Ham and Japheth built upon the sea shore, and the
banks of great rivers. But the exile of the Jews converted
them necessarily into merchants. Denied as a general rule
citizenship in the land of their refuge, subject at any moment to spoliation and expulsion, their only sure means of
living was in traffic, in which they soon became skilled on
the principles of a specialty in labor.

They naturally, therefore, followed in their dispersion,
as they have ever since done, the great channels of commerce throughout the world, with such deflections here and
there as persecution rendered necessary. But notwithstanding the many impulses to which their wanderings have been
subjected, they have in the main obeyed the general laws
of migration by moving east and west upon nearly the same

parallels of latitude. Their numbers in spite of losses by
all causes, including religious defection, which, everything
considered, has been remarkably small, have steadily in-
creased and are now variously estimated at seven to nine
millions. They may be divided, says Dr. Pressell, into three
great classes, the enumeration of which will show their
wonderful dispersion. The first of these inhabit the interior
of Africa, Arabia, India, China, Turkestan and Bokhara.
Even the Arabs, Mr. Disraeli terms Jews upon horseback;
they are however, the sons of Ishmael—half-brothers to the
Jews. These are the lowest of the Jewish people in wealth,
intelligence and religion, though said to be superior to their
Gentile neighbors in each. The second and most numerous
class is found in Northern Africa, Egypt, Palestine, Syria,
Mesopotamia, Persia, Asia Minor, European Turkey, Poland, Russia and parts of Austria. In these are found the
strictly orthodox, Talmudical Jews; the sect *Chasidim*, who
are the representatives of the Zealots of Josephus, and the
small but most interesting sect Karaites, who reject all Rabbinical traditions, and are the only Jews who adhere to the
strict letter of the Scriptures. This class is represented as
being very ignorant of all except Jewish learning—it being
prohibited to study any other. Yet they alone are regarded
by scholars as the proper expounders of ancient Talmudical
Judaism. As might be inferred from the character of the
governments under which they live, their political condition is most unhappy and insecure, and their increase in
wealth and their social progress are slow. The third and
last class are those of Central and Western Europe, and
the United States. These are by far the most intelligent and
civilized of their race, not only keeping pace with the progress of their Gentile neighbors, but contributing to it
largely. Their Oriental mysticism seems to have given
place to the stronger practical ideas of Western Europe,
with which they have come in contact, and they have em-

braced them fully. They are denominated "reforming" in their tenets, attempting to eliminate the Talmudical traditions which cumber and obscure their creed, and adapt it somewhat to the spirit of the age, though in tearing this away, they have also, say the theologians, dispensed with much of the Old Testament itself. In fact, they have become simply Unitarians or Deists.

Many curious facts concerning them are worthy to be noted. In various cities of the Eastern World they have been for ages, and in some are yet, huddled into crowded and filthy streets or quarters, in a manner violative of all the rules of health, yet it is a notorious fact that they have ever suffered less from pestilential diseases than their Christian neighbors. So often have the black wings of epidemic plagues passed over them, and smitten all around them, that ignorance and malignity frequently accused them of poisoning the wells and fountains and of exercising sorcery.

They have also in a very noticeable degree been exempt from consumption and all diseases of the respiratory functions, which in them are said by physicians to be wonderfully adapted to enduring the vicissitudes of all temperatures and climates. The average duration of Gentile life is computed at 26 years—it certainly does not reach 30; that of the Jew, according to a most interesting table of statistics which I have seen, is full 37 years. The number of infants born to the married couple exceeds that to the Gentile races, and the number dying in infancy is much smaller. In height they are nearly three inches lower than the average of other races; the width of their bodies with outstretched arms is one inch shorter than the height, whilst in other races it is eight inches longer on the average. But on the other hand, the length of the trunk is much greater with the Jew, in proportion to height than with other races. In the Negro the trunk constitutes 32 per cent of the height of the whole body, in the European 34 per cent, in the Jew

36 per cent. What these physical peculiarities have had to do with their wonderful preservation and steady increase, I leave for the philosophers to explain.

Their social life is, if possible, still more remarkable. There is neither prostitution nor pauperism, and but little abject poverty among them. They have some paupers, it is true but they trouble neither you nor me. Crime in the malignant, wilful sense of that word is exceedingly rare. I have never known but one Jew convicted of any offense beyond the grade of a misdemeanor, though I am free to say, I have known many a one who would have been improved by a little hanging. They contribute liberally to all Gentile charities in the communities where they live; they ask nothing from the Gentiles for their own. If a Jew is broken down in business, the others set him up again or give him employment and his children have bread. If one is in trouble the others stand by him with counsel and material aid, remembering the command, "Thou shalt open thine hand wide unto thy brethren, and shall surely lend him sufficient for his need, in that which he wanteth." Their average education is far ahead of the races by whom they are surrounded. I have never seen an adult Jew who could not read, write and compute figures—*especially the figures*. Of the four great human industries which conduce to the public wealth, agriculture, manufacturing, mining and commerce, as a general rule they engage only in one. They are neither farmers, miners, smiths, carpenters, mechanics or artisans of any kind. They are merchants only, but as such, own few or no ships, and they are rarely carriers of any kind. They wander over the whole earth, but they are never pioneers, and they found no colonies, because as I suppose, being devoted to one business only, they lack the self-sustaining elements of those who build new states; and whilst they engage individually in politics where they are not disfranchised, and contend for offices and honors like other people, they yet seek nowhere *political power or national aggregation.* Dealers in every kind of merchandise, with rare exceptions they manufacture none. They dwell exclusively in towns, cities and villages, but as a general rule do not own the property they live upon. They marry within themselves entirely, and yet in defiance of well known natural laws, with regard to breeding "in and in," their race does not degenerate. With them family government is perhaps more supreme than with any other people. Divorce, domestic discord, and disobedience to parents are almost unknown among them.

The process by which they have become the leading merchants, bankers, and financiers of the world is explained by their history. In many places their children were not permitted to enter the schools, or even to be enrolled in the guilds of labor. Trade was therefore the only avenue left open to them. In most countries they dared not or could not own the soil. Why a nation of original agriculturists ceased to cultivate the soil altogether is therefore only seemingly inexplicable. All nations must have a certain proportion of their population engaged in tilling the soil; as the Jews have no common country they reside in all; and in all countries they have the shrewdness to see that whilst it is most honorable to plow, yet all men live more comfortably than the plowman. In addition to which, as before intimated, agriculture so fixed them to the soil that it would have been impossible to evade persecution and spoliation. They were constantly on the move, and their wealth must therefore be portable and easily secreted—hence their early celebrity as lapidaries, dealers in diamonds and precious stones—and hence too, their introduction of *bills of exchange*. The utility of these great aids to commerce had long been known to the world—perhaps by both Greek and Roman—but could never be made available by them, because confidence in the integrity of each other did not exist between the drawer and the drawee. But this integrity, which the lordly merchants of the Christian and the Pagan world could not inspire, was found to exist in the persecuted and despised Jew. So much for the lessons of adversity. These arts diligently applied, at first from necessity, afterwards from choice, in the course of centuries made the Jews skillful above all men in the ways of merchandise and money changing, and finally developed in them those peculiar faculties and aptitudes for a calling which are brought out as well in man by the special education of successive generations, as in the lower animals. The Jew merchant had this advantage, too, that whereas his Gentile competitor belonged to a *consolidated nation*, confined to certain geographical limits, speaking a certain tongue, the aid, sympathy and influence which he derived from social and political ties, were also confined to the limits of his nation. But the Jew merchant belonged to a *scattered nation*, spread out over the whole earth, speaking many tongues, and welded together, not by social ties alone, but by the fierce fires of suffering and persecution; and the aid, sympathy, influence and information which he derived therefrom came out of the utmost parts of the earth.

When after many centuries the flames of persecution had abated so that the Jews were permitted more than bare life, their industry, energy and talent soon placed them among the important motive powers of the world. They entered the fields of commerce in its grandest and most colossal operations. They became the friends and counselors of kings, the prime-ministers of empires, the treasurers of republics, the movers of armies, the arbiters of public credit, the patrons of art, and the critics of literature. We do not forget the time in the near past when the peace of Europe —of three worlds hung upon the Jewish Prime-Minister of England. No people are so ready to accommodate themselves to circumstances. It was but recently that we heard of an English Jew taking an absolute lease of the ancient Persian Empire. The single family of Rothschild, the progeny of a poor German Jew, who three generations ago sold curious old coins under the sign of a *red shield*, are now the possessors of greater wealth and power than was Solomon, when he could send 1,300,000 fighting men into the field!

Twenty years ago, when this family was in the height of its power, perhaps no sovereign in Europe could have waged a successful war against its united will. Two centuries since the ancestors of these Jewish money-kings were skulking in the caverns of the earth or hiding in the squalid outskirts of persecuting cities. Nor let it be supposed that it is in this field alone we see the great effects of Jewish intellect and energy. The genius which showed itself capable of controlling the financial affairs of the world, necessarily carried with it other great powers and capabilities. The Jews in fact, under most adverse circumstances, made their mark—a high and noble mark—in every other department of human affairs. Christian clergymen have sat at the feet of their Rabbis to be taught the mystic learning of the East; Senates have been enrapt by the eloquence of Jewish orators; courts have been convinced by the acumen and learning of Jewish lawyers; vast throngs excited to the wildest enthusiasm by Jewish histrionic and aesthetic art; Jewish science has helped to number the stars in their courses, to loose the bands of Orion and to guide Arcturus with his sons.

Jewish literature has delighted and instructed all classes of mankind and the world has listened with rapture and with tears to Jewish melody and song. For never since its spirit was evoked under the shadow of the vines on the hills of Palestine to soothe the melancholy of her King, has Judah's harp, whether in freedom or captivity, in sorrow or joy, ceased to wake the witchery of its tuneful strings.

Time forbids that I should even name the greatest of those who have distinguished themselves and made good their claim to rank with the foremost of earth. No section of the human family can boast a greater list of men and women entitled to be placed among the true children of genius—going to make up the primacy of our race—in every branch of human affairs, in every phase of human civilization. Mr. Draper says that for four hundred years of the middle ages—ages more dark and terrible to them than to any others, they took the most philosophical and comprehensive view of things of all European people.

On the whole, and after due deliberation, I think it may be truthfully said, that there is more of average wealth, intelligence, and morality among the Jewish people than there is among any other nation of equal numbers in the world! If this be true—if it be half true—when we consider the circumstances under which it has all been brought about, it constitutes in the eyes of thinking men the most remarkable moral phenomenon ever exhibited by any portion of the human family. For not only has the world given the Jew no help, but all that he is, he has made himself in spite of the world—in spite of its bitter cruelty, its scorn and unspeakable tyranny. The most he has ever asked, certainly the most he has ever received, and that but rarely, *was to be left alone.* To escape the sword, the rack, the fire, and utter spoiling of his goods, has indeed, for centuries, been to him a blessed heritage, as the shadow of a great rock in a weary land.

The physical persecution of the Jews has measurably ceased among all nations of the highest civilization. There is no longer any proscription left upon their political rights in any land where the English tongue is spoken. I am proud of the fact. But there remains among us an unreasonable prejudice of which I am heartily ashamed. Our toleration will not be complete until we put it away also, as well as the old implements of physical torture.

This age, and these United States in particular, so boastful of toleration, presents some curious evidences of the fact that the old spirit is not dead; evidences tending much to show that the prejudices of 2000 years ago are still with

A forerunner of W.W. II persecution this was 1880 or 1890

us. In Germany, a land more than all others indebted to the genius and loyal energy of the Jews, a vast uprising against them was lately excited for the sole reason, so far as one can judge, that they occupy too many places of learning and honor, and are becoming too rich!

In this, our own free and tolerant land, where wars have been waged and constitutions violated for the benefit of the African negro, the descendants of barbarian tribes who for 4000 years have contributed nothing to, though in close contact with the civilization of mankind, save as the Helots contributed an example to the Spartan youth, and where laws and partisan courts alike have been used to force him into an equality with those whom he could not equal, we have seen Jews, educated and respectable men, descendants of those from whom we derive our civilization, kinsmen, after the flesh, of Him whom we esteem as the Son of God and Saviour of men, ignominiously ejected from hotels and watering places as unworthy the association of men who had grown rich by the sale of a new brand of soap or an improved patent rat-trap!

I have never heard of one of these indecent thrusts at the Jews without thinking of the dying words of Sergeant Bothwell when he saw his life's current dripping from the sword of Burley: "Base peasant churl, thou hast spilt the blood of a line of Kings."

Let us learn to judge the Jew as we judge other men— *by his merits*. And above all, let us cease the abominable injustice of holding the *class* responsible for the sins of the *individual*. We apply this test to no other people.

Our principal excuse for disliking him now is that we have injured him. The true gentleman, Jew or Gentile, will always recognize the true gentleman, Jew or Gentile, and will refuse to consort with an ill-bred impostor, Jew or Gentile, simply because he is an ill-bred impostor.

The impudence of the low-bred Jew is not one whit more detestable than the impudence of the low-bred Gentile, children of shoddy, who by countless thousands swarm into doors opened for them by our democracy. Let us cry quits on that score. Let us judge each other by our best not our worst samples, and when we find gold let us recognize it. Let us prove all things and hold fast that which is good.

Whilst it is a matter of just pride to us that there is neither physical persecution nor legal proscription left upon the civil rights of the Jews in any land where the English tongue is spoken or the English law obtains, yet I consider it a grave reproach not only to us, but to all christendom that such injustice is permitted anywhere. The recent barbarities inflicted upon them in Russia revive the recollection of the darkest cruelties of the middle ages. That is one crying outrage, one damned spot that blackens the fair light of the nineteenth century, without the semblance of excuse or the shadow of justification. That glare of burning homes, those shrieks of outraged women, those wailings of orphaned children go up to God, not only as witnesses against the wretched savages who perpetrate them, but as accusations also of those who permit them. How sad it is again to hear that old cry of Jewish sorrow, which we had hoped to hear no more forever! How shameful it is to know that within the shadow of so-called Christian churches, there are yet dark places filled with the habitations of cruelty. No considerations of diplomacy or international courtesy should for one moment stand in the way of their stern and instant suppression.

The Jews are our spiritual fathers, the authors of our morals, the founders of our civilization with all the power and dominion arising therefrom, and the great peoples professing Christianity and imbued with any of its noble spirit, should see to it that justice and protection are afforded them. By simply speaking with one voice it could be done, for no power on earth could resist that voice. Every consideration of humanity and international policy demands it. Their unspeakable misfortunes, their inherited woes, their very helplessness appeal to our Christian chivalry, trumpet-tongued in behalf of those wretched victims of a prejudice for which tolerant Christianity is not altogether irresponsible.

There are objections to the Jew as a citizen; many objections; some true and some false, some serious and some trivial. It is said that industrially he produces nothing, invents nothing, adds nothing to the public wealth; that he will not own real estate, nor take upon himself those permanent ties which beget patriotism and become the hostages of good citizenship; that he merely *sojourns* in the land and does not *dwell in it*, but is ever in light marching order and is ready to flit when the word comes to go. These are true objections in the main, and serious ones, but I submit the fault is not his, even here.

> "Quoth old Mazeppa, ill-betide
> The school wherein I learned to ride."

These habits he learned by persecution. He dwelt everywhere in fear and trembling, and had no assurance of his life. He was ever ready to leave because at any moment he might be compelled to choose between leaving and death. He built no house, because at any moment he and his little ones might be thrust out of it to perish. He cherished no love for the land because it cherished none for him, but was cruel and hard and bitter to him. And yet history shows that in every land where he has been protected he has been a faithful and zealous patriot. Also since his rights have been secured he has begun to show the same permanent attachments to the soil as other people, and is rapidly building houses and in some places cultivating farms. These objections he is rapidly removing since we have removed their cause.

So, too, the impression is sought to be made that he is dishonest in his dealings with the Gentiles, insincere in his professions, servile to his superiors and tyrannical to his

inferiors, oriental in his habits and manner. That the Jew
—meaning the *class*—is dishonest, I believe to be an atro-
cious calumny; and, considering that we derive all of our
notions of rectitude from the Jew, who first taught the
world that command, "Thou shalt not steal," and "Thou
shalt not bear false witness," we pay ourselves a shabby
compliment in thus befouling our teachers. Undoubtedly
there are Jewish scoundrels in great abundance; undoubtedly also there are Gentile scoundrels in greater abundance.
Southern reconstruction put that fact beyond a peradventure. But our own scoundrels are *orthodox*, Jewish scoundrels are *unbelievers*—*that* is the difference. If a man robs
me I should thank him that he denies my creed too; he com-
pliments both me and it by the denial.

The popular habit is to regard an injury done to one by
a man of different creed as a double wrong; to me it seems
that the wrong is the greater coming from my own. To hold
also, as some do, that the sins of all people are due to their
creeds, would leave the sins of the sinners of my creed quite
unaccounted for. With some the faith of a scoundrel is all
important; it is not so with me.

All manner of crimes, including perjury, cheating and
over-reaching in trade, are unhesitatingly attributed to the
Jews, generally by their rivals in trade. Yet somehow they
are rarely proven to the satisfaction of even Gentile judges
and juries. The gallows clutches but few, nor are they found
in the jails and penitentiaries—a species of real estate which
I honor them for not investing in. I admit that there was
and is perhaps now a remnant of the feeling that it was legal
to spoil the Egyptians. Their constant life of persecution
would naturally inspire this feeling; their *present* life of
toleration and their business estimate of the value of character will as naturally remove it. Again and again, day by
day, we evince our Gentile superiority in the tricks of trade
and sharp practice. It is asserted by our proverbial exclama-
tion in regard to a particular piece of villainy, "That beats

the Jews!" And I call your attention to the further fact that, sharp as they undoubtedly are, they have found it impossible to make a living in New England. Outside of Boston, not fifty perhaps can be found in all that land of unsuspecting integrity and modest righteousness. They have managed to endure with longsuffering patience the knout of the Czar and the bowstring of the Turk, but they have fled for life from the presence of the wooden nutmegs and the left-handed gimlets of Jonathan. Is there any man who hears me tonight who, if a Yankee and a Jew were to "lock horns" in a regular encounter of commercial wits, would not give large odds on the Yankee? My own opinion is that the genuine "guessing" Yankee, with a jack-knife and a pine shingle could in two hours time whittle the smartest Jew in New York out of his homestead in the Abrahamic covenant.

I agreed with Lord Macaulay that the Jew is what we have made him. If he is a bad job, in all honesty we should contemplate him as the handiwork of our own civilization. If there be indeed guile upon his lips or servility in his manner, we should remember that such are the legitimate fruits of oppression and wrong, and that they have been, since the pride of Judah was broken and his strength scattered, his only means of turning aside the uplifted sword and the poised javelin of him who sought to plunder and slay. Indeed so long has he schemed and shifted to avoid injustice and cruelty, that we can perceive in him all the restless watchfulness which characterizes the hunted animal.

To this day the cast of the Jew's features in repose is habitually grave and sad as though the very ploughshare of sorrow had marked its furrows across their faces forever.

"And where shall Israel lave her bleeding feet?
And when shall Zion's songs again seem sweet,
And Judah's melody once more rejoice
The hearts that leaped before its heavenly voice?
Tribes of the wandering foot and weary heart

How shall ye flee away and be at rest?
The wild dove hath her nest—the fox his cave—
Mankind their country—Israel but the grave."
Many only made the open grovel!

The hardness of Christian prejudice having dissolved, so will that of the Jew. The hammer of persecution having ceased to beat upon the iron mass of their stubbornness, *it* will cease to consolidate and harden, and the main strength of their exclusion and preservation will have been lost. They will perhaps learn that one sentence of our Lord's prayer, which it is said is not to be found in the Talmud, and which is the key-note of the difference between Jew and Gentile, "Forgive us our trespasses *as we* forgive them who trespass against us."

If so, they will become as other men, and taking their harps down from the willows, no longer refuse to sing the songs of Zion because they are captives in a strange land.

I believe that there is a morning to open yet for the Jews in Heaven's good time, and if that opening shall be in any way commensurate with the darkness of the night through which they have passed, it will be the brightest that ever dawned upon a faithful people.

I have stood on the summit of the very monarch of our great Southern Alleghanies and seen the night flee away before the chariot wheels of the God of day. The stars receded before the pillars of lambent fire that pierced the zenith, a thousand ragged mountain peaks began to peer up from the abysmal darkness, each looking through the vapory seas that filled the gorges like an island whose "jutting and confounded base was swilled by the wild and wasteful ocean." As the curtain was lifted more and more and the eastern brightness grew in radiance and in glory, animate nature prepared to receive her Lord; the tiny snowbird from its nest in the turf began chirping to its young; the silver pheasant sounded its morning drum-beat for its mate in the boughs of the fragrant fir; the dun deer rising slowly from his mossy couch and stretching himself in graceful curves, began to crop the tender herbage; whilst the lordly eagle rising straight upward from his home on the crag, with pinions wide spread, bared his golden breast to the yellow beams and screamed his welcome to the sun in his coming! Soon the vapors of the night are lifted up on shafts of fire, rolling and seething in billows of refulgent flame, until when far overhead, they are caught upon the wings of the morning breeze and swept away, perfect day was established and there was peace. So may it be with this long-suffering and immortal people. So may the real spirit of Christ yet be so triumphantly infused amongst those who profess to obey his teachings, that with one voice and one hand they will stay the persecutions and hush the sorrows of these their wondrous kinsmen, put them forward into the places of honor and the homes of love where all the lands in which they dwell, shall be to them as was Jerusalem to their fathers. So may the morning come, not to them alone, but to all the children of men who, through much tribulation and with heroic manhood have waited for its dawning, with a faith whose constant cry through all the dreary watches of the night has been, "Though he slay me, yet will I trust in him!"

"Roll golden sun, roll swiftly toward the west,
    Dawn happy day when many woes shall cease;
Come quickly Lord, thy people wait the rest
    Of thine abiding peace!

No more, no more to hunger here for love;
    No more to thirst for blessings long denied.
Judah! Thy face is foul with weeping, but above
    Thou shalt be satisfied!"

Appendices

APPENDIX A

First Memorial Ceremony at Charlotte

Excerpts from report about memorial ceremony on April 16, 1894, at Charlotte, on the day before the funeral of Zebulon B. Vance, at Asheville, from *The Charlotte Observer*:

Beautiful and touching speeches were made but the gem of all was that of the long time law partner of the dead Senator [Clement Dowd]. His voice was full of tears, his whole being quivering with sincere and ill-suppressed emotion, and it almost seemed that drops of blood from his lacerated heart lingered about the words which fell from his lips. He said: "If I should say this bereavement came as a personal one to me I should only say what was true of every man, woman and child in the State, for the Governor was loved by all. No man before him was ever so universally loved. His image seemed to be engraved upon the hearts of all his people. He was especially the friend of the common people, even little children instinctively knew he was their friend." The speaker told of two country men, who during the late campaign inquired of him whether Vance was coming to Charlotte. No, was the reply; he is not strong enough to speak. "Oh, we don't want him to speak. We just want to see him one more time," said one. "I would ride ten miles through the rain the worst day in the winter just to get to see the side of his face," said the other.

"No one thoroughly knew him," continued the speaker. "I did not. He was not built to the measure of other men. He was a great reader and student of history. He loved old books and ancient stories and characters. He was fond of taking Cyrus, Alexander, Cæsar, Hannibal, and getting the gist of their campaigns, comparing them with similar campaigns of modern times. He even found time to make detours into astronomy and geology. He had many adversaries; he was in many battles and conflicts, but I don't think he had an enemy when he died. In his great big heart there was no place for enmity. His life was pure, and no scandal was ever attached to his name. They will lay him to rest among the mountains where his boyhood and early life were spent, and from that lofty couch he will be among the very first to catch the dawn of the eternal day."

This surpassingly eloquent peroration was greeted with an unsuppressed and uncontrollable outburst of applause, which, yet at the same time seemed somehow to be muffled and in mourning.

The Rev. Dr. Preston, pastor of the First Presbyterian church, said he thought one of the most remarkable things about this remarkable man, and which made most for his remarkable career, was the training of his mother. She had laid the foundation for his character and reputation to rest upon. He pictured the Governor in his old pew in the First Presbyterian church in former days; he was not a communicant then, but had the knowledge of his mother's training as a holy inspiration, but it was not till after the death of his wife that he connected himself with any church; that most appalling family affliction, the greatest calamity that can befall any man, was the chart and compass which guided him to port. Governor Vance was then found, not uniting with some strong church, but with a little struggling church in Raleigh, and recently, when occasion came to remove his membership, he placed it in the old church in Charlotte, so fragrant to him, doubtless, with sweet associations.

Perhaps there was never before a memorial meeting held in honor of a great Gentile prince at which an Israelite stood up and paid such a tribute as did Mr. Samuel Wittkowsky to the memory of Zebulon B. Vance. He spoke of how Vance had won the hearts of the Hebrews of this State and country by the full measure of justice he accorded them in his famous lecture on the "Scattered Nation," and he said no

Israelite ever voted against Vance. Such a blow has fallen upon our State and country that it will take long years to overcome it. In common with the million and a half of North Carolina's sons and daughters I wish to give expression not only to my feelings personally on this melancholy event, but I speak also for my race in the State and throughout the Union. The deceased has ever by his words and acts demonstrated that he was their friend. And now, fellow-citizens, let us perpetuate his memory and teach our children to instruct their children and their children's children to revere his memory, and that wherever their lot may be cast and they are asked where they came from, to point with pride to the State which gave birth to Zebulon B. Vance.

The next speaker was Col. Hamilton C. Jones, and his was a very beautiful tribute, indeed, and deserves a full report which a lack of time forbids. He related among other things that after Vance had been elected to the United States Senate, while Governor of the State, and was about leaving for Washington, I saw him and said this honor must be very pleasing and gratifying to you, and he replied as God is my judge, be assured I would rather serve the people as Governor than to be the foremost Senator in the United States. Col. Jones said Senator Vance was easily first among all the statesmen North Carolina had produced; that he did not understand the art of mere politics. His triumphs came from honest purpose and right conviction.

where are the ones of this philosophy in outline?

As reported in Dowd, Clement, *Life of Zebulon B. Vance* (Charlotte, 1897), p. 321.

Second Memorial Ceremony at Charlotte

Excerpts from report about memorial ceremony on April 18, 1894, at Charlotte, on the day after the funeral of Zebulon B. Vance at Asheville, from *The Daily Observer*:

"Vance, of, by and for the people," said Capt. Ardrey yesterday.

Surely no man was ever loved as this one. Country and town assembled yesterday to do honor to his memory.

The auditorium held between two and three thousand people. An audience composed of high and low, rich and poor, country and town people. Just such an assemblage has not been seen here before. The country people began coming in early yesterday morning. Every township in the county was represented. All came with like impulse and sentiment—with fervid desire to pay tribute to "Zeb Vance," the people's idol.

There were on the rostrum, besides the singers, Rev. Dr. Preston, Major C. Dowd, Capt. W. E. Ardrey, Major S. W. Reid, Dr. J. B. Alexander, Col. J. E. Brown, Messrs. J. M. Kirkpatrick, C. W. Tillett, J. P. Alexander, John Springs Davidson, H. K. Reid, and J. Hervy Henderson.

. . .

After the hymn, Capt. W. E. Ardrey addressed the audience.

"We have met," said he, "to do honor to a great man. This meeting was called in honor of our great Senator, Zebulon B. Vance. He was of the people, by the people and for the people, and he lives in the hearts of the people. It is a delight to honor this great and glorious man. While North Carolina has its Gastons, Grahams and others, she can boast of only one Zeb Vance. He was her great leader.

Wherever he lead the people followed. He had no will of his own when her interests were at stake. His bidding was from God and his country. He was poor because he was honest. His name will be handed down with that of Webster, Calhoun and other great men. Whoever his mantel falls on will receive a pure and spotless one. We thank God to-day, my friends, that he died with clean hands and a pure heart. Let us teach our children to honor and revere the name of Zebulon Baird Vance."

· · ·

Mr. John Springs Davidson was the next speaker. He paid an enthusiastic and loving tribute to Senator Vance. "It is the duty of every citizen in the United States to pay tribute to Senator Vance," said he. "If God had spared his life he would have occupied the highest position in the gift of the people. [Great applause]. I say to the young men of Mecklenburg to take Zeb Vance as their model. There may be a Zeb Vance in this audience. Emulate his example. He was the greatest man of this day and of this generation."

· · ·

Mr. J. P. Alexander next paid his tribute to Vance. He dwelt particularly on the war record of the great war Governor. "Where is the State," said he, "that has produced another Vance, or any one like him? There was no Mason's and Dixon's line separating the good will of the people. The North honored him as well as did the South. He was the greatest man America has ever produced."

· · ·

The gem of all the talks was reserved for the last—that of Mr. C. W. Tillett. From the moment he repeated the first sad words—"Zeb Vance is dead"—through every tear-bedimmed utterance, the people sat enrapt, and handkerchief after handkerchief went faceward to catch the falling tears:

"Zeb Vance is dead! Few and short are these cruel words which men with lips compressed and cheeks all blanched have whispered one to another; and yet they bear the message of the greatest grief which ever yet has filled the Old North State.

"Zeb Vance is dead! Ring out the funeral bells and let their mournful tones re-echo in the empty chambers of the hearts once filled with gladsome sounds of his loved voice.

"Zeb Vance is dead! And mirth herself hath put on mourning; and laughter, child of his most genial brain, hath hid her face in tears.

"Zeb Vance is dead! The fires of party strife are quenched; and throbbing hearts and tear-beclouded eyes tell more than words of grandest eloquence the anguish of the people's minds and how they loved him.

"Zeb Vance is dead! Soldier, statesman, patriot, friend! In war and peace, the one of all her sons to whom his mother State looked most for succor and relief; and can it be that in the days to come, when dreaded dangers threaten all around, we nevermore can call for him before whose matchless powers in days gone by our enemies have quailed and fled?

"Zeb Vance is dead! His was a name you could conjure with, and oftimes in the past, when this loved Commonwealth of ours has been stirred to its inmost depths, and men knew not which way to go nor what to say, the cry was sounded forth that 'Vance is coming,' and from the mountain fastness of the west and the everglades of the eastern plains, the people came who never would come forth to hear another living man, and gathering around in countless multitudes, they hung upon his every word with eager eye and listening ear, and all he told them they believed because 'our Vance' had said it.

"Zeb Vance is dead! And where shall come the man to tell the world soul-inspiring story of his hero life? How, coming forth from humble home, he baffled and o'ercame the fates that would have crushed beneath their feet a man of meaner mould; how serving faithfully and well in every trust committed unto him, he soon won first place in the hearts of all his countrymen and held that place for three score years unto the end; how, when his native land was plunged in throes of civil strife, he went forth in the front rank to defend and save her and fought with valor all her foes; how called to rule as chief executive in times that tried men's souls, he ruled so wisely and so well; how when the war was over and the cause was lost—when down upon his bleeding, prostrate country came the horde of vampires from the North to suck the last remaining drops of life blood from his people, he rose with power almost divine and drove them back; and then with gentle hand he caused the wounds to heal and his loved land to prosper once again as in the years gone by; and how at last, when after years of faithful, honest toil, upon his noble form was laid the icy hand of death, he bowed his head in meek submission to His will and yielded up to God his manly soul! Who can be found to sing the praise of such a one, and who can speak the anguish of the people's hearts at his untimely death?

"Zeb Vance is dead! He was the friend and tribune of the people. Though he rose to place where he held converse with the great and mighty of the earth, his sympathetic heart was open wide to all mankind, and his strong arm was first stretched forth to lift the lowliest of the sons of men that cried to him for help, and in the Nation's Senate halls his voice was ever lifted up to plead the cause of the down-trodden and oppressed against the favored classes and the money kings.

"Zeb Vance is dead! And when he died, a poor man died; for though he stood where oft there was within his grasp the gains of millions if he would but swerve from right and reach it, he cast it all aside with scorn, and dying, left his sons and all the people of his land the priceless legacy of an honest and untarnished name.

"Zeb Vance is dead! And yet he lives; the influence of his noble words and honest life can never die; and in the years to come men gathering round their firesides at the evening hour shall tell their sons of him and how he scorned a lie and scorned dishonest gains.

"Zeb Vance is dead! But he shall live forever more. Oh, blessed truth, which Mary's Son, the God-man, taught when standing near the tomb with His all-conquering foot upon the skull of death, He called forth Lazarus unto life, and told a listening world the thrilling truth that whosoever lived and in His name believed should never die.

"Zeb Vance is dead! If it be truth

'That men may rise on stepping stones
Of their dead selves to higher things,'

"Oh, grander truth, that a nation too may rise on stepping stones of her dead hero sons unto a higher life. And God vouchsafe that our own State, while weeping o'er the grave of him, her best-loved, most honored son, may yet be thereby lifted into a grander, nobler life."

As reported in Dowd, p. 323.

Eulogies in the United States Senate

A memorial ceremony was held in the United States Senate on January 19, 1895. Nine Senators delivered eulogies. Among them was Senator Matt W. Ransom from North Carolina. These eulogies were in addition to those delivered at the time of Vance's decease on April 14, 1894. Excerpts from Senator Ransom's address:

[Address of Mr. Ransom.]

MR. PRESIDENT: The Senate is asked to render its last duties of honor and sorrow to the memory of the Hon. Zebulon Baird Vance, late a Senator from North Carolina.

In this Chamber on the 16th of last April, two days after his death, the Senate lighted its black torches around the lifeless form of that most honored and beloved son of our State, and his mortal figure, covered with the white flowers of spring and love, and hallowed by the sacred devotions of religion, passed amid tears like a shadow from these portals forever. To-day his associates on this floor are here to place on the ever-living annals of the Senate the record of their admiration and affection for his virtues.

In 1878 he was elected to the Senate, and until he died remained a member of this body, having been elected four times a Senator. His record in the Senate is part of the nation's history. From the beginning he was an active, earnest debater, a constant, faithful worker, a dutiful, devoted Senator, aspiring and laboring for the welfare and honor of the whole country. He was at all times on the important committees of the body, and took a prominent part in the discussion of almost every leading question. He was the unceasing advocate of revenue reform, uncompromisingly opposed to civil service, and the ardent friend of silver money and its free coinage by the Government.

He vigilantly defended the rights, honor, and interests of the Southern States, not from sectional passion or prejudice, but because it was his duty as a patriot to every State and to the Union. He was bold, brave, open, candid, and without reserve. He desired all the world to know his opinions and positions and never hesitated to avow them.

His heart every moment was in North Carolina. His devotion to the State and people was unbounded; his solicitude for her welfare, his deep anxiety in all that concerned her, and his ever readiness to make every sacrifice in her behalf was daily manifested in all his words and actions. Senator Vance was an uncommon orator. He spoke with great power. His style was brief, clear, and strong. His statements were accurate and definite, his arguments compact and forcible, his illustrations unsurpassed in their fitness. His wit and humor were the ever-waiting and ready handmaids to his reasoning, and always subordinated to the higher purpose of his speech. They were torchbearers, ever bringing fresh light. He always instructed, always interested, always entertained, and never wearied or fatigued an audience, and knew when to conclude. The Senate always heard him with pleasure, and the occupants of the galleries hung upon his lips, and with bended bodies and outstretched necks would catch his every word as it fell.

He rarely, if ever, spoke without bringing down applause. His wit was as inexhaustible as it was exquisite. His humor was overflowing, fresh, sparkling like bubbling drops of wine in a goblet; but he husbanded these rare resources of speech with admirable skill, and never displayed them for ostentation. They were weapons of offense and defense, and were always kept sharp and bright and ready for use. He was master of irony and sarcasm, but there was no malice, no hatred in his swift and true arrows. Mortal wounds were often given, but the shafts were never poisoned. It was the strength of the bow and the skill of the archer that sent the steel through the heart of its victim.

But strength, force, clearness, brevity, honesty of conviction, truth, passion, good judgment, were the qualities that made his speech powerful and effective.

He believed what he said. He knew it was true; he felt its force himself; his heart was in his words; he was ready to put place, honor, life itself, upon the issue. This was the secret of his popularity, fame, and success as a speaker. He studied his speeches with the greatest care, deliberated, meditated upon them constantly, arranged the order of his topics with consummate discretion, introduced authorities from history, and very often from sacred history, presented some popular faith as an anchor to his ship, and concluded with a sincere appeal to the patriotic impulses of the people. No speaker ever resorted to the bayonet more frequently.

He did not skirmish; he marched into the battle, charged the center of the lines, and never failed to draw the blood of the enemy. Sometimes he was supreme in manner, in words, in thought, in pathos. He possessed the thunderbolts, but, like Jove, he never trifled with them; he only invoked them when gigantic perils confronted his cause. In 1876, upon his third nomination for Governor, speaking to an immense audience in the State-house Square at Raleigh, he held up both hands in the light of the sun and with solemn invocation to Almighty God declared that they were white and stainless, that not one cent of corrupt money had ever touched their palms. The effect was electric; the statement was conviction and conclusion. The argument was unanswerable. It was great nature's action. It was eloquence. It was truth.

Senator Vance's integrity and uprightness in public and in private life were absolute; they were unimpeached and unimpeachable; he was honest; it is the priceless inheritance which he leaves to his family, his friends, his country. He was an honest man. Calumny fell harmless at his feet; the light dissipated every cloud and he lived continually in its broad rays; his breastplate, his shield, his armor was the light, the truth. There was no darkness, no mystery, no shadow upon his bright standard.

·   ·   ·

He had not the wisdom and virtue of Macon; he was not like Badger, a master of argument, he was not like Graham, a model of dignity and learning; he had not the superb speech and grand passion of Mangum; he wanted the tenacious and inexorable logic of Bragg; but in all the endowments, qualities, faculties, and attainments that make up the orator and the statesmen he was the equal of either. No man among the living or the dead has ever so possessed and held the hearts of North Carolina's people. In their confidence, their affection, their devotion, and their gratitude he stood unapproachable—without a peer. When he spoke to them they listened to him with faith, with admiration, with rapture and exultant joy. His name was ever upon their lips. His pictures were in almost every household. Their children by hundreds bore his beloved name, and his words of wit and wisdom were repeated by every tongue.

What Tell was to Switzerland, what Bruce was to Scotland, what William of Orange was to Holland, I had almost said what Moses was to Israel, Vance was to North Carolina. I can give you but a faint idea of the deep, fervid, exalted sentiment which our people cherished for their greatest tribune. He was of them. He was one of them. He was with them. His thoughts, his feelings, his words were theirs. He was their shepherd, their champion, their friend, their guide, blood of their blood, great, good, noble, true, human like they were in all respects, no better, but wiser, abler, with higher knowledge and profounder learning.

Nor was this unsurpassed devotion unreasonable or without just foundation. For more than the third of a century, for upward of thirty years, in peace and in war, in prosperity and in adversity, in joy and in sorrow, he had stood by them like a brother—a defender, a preserver, a deliverer. He was their martyr and had suffered for their acts. He was their shield and had protected them from evil and from peril. He had been with them—he had been with them and their sons and brothers on the march, by the camp fires, in the burning light of battle; beside the wounded and the dying; in their darkest hours, amid hunger and cold, and famine and pestilences, his watchful care had brought them comfort and shelter and protection. They remembered the gray jackets, the warm blankets, the good shoes, the timely food, the blessed medicines, which his sympathy and provision had brought them. In defeat, amid tumult, amid ruin, humiliation, and the loss of all they had, he had been their adviser; he had guided them through the wilderness of their woes and brought them safely back to their rights and all their hopes. He had been to them like the north star to the storm-tossed and despairing mariner. He had been greater than Ulysses to the Greeks. He had preserved their priceless honor, had saved their homes, and was the defender of their liberties. He was their benefactor. Every object around them reminded them of his care, every memory recalled, every thought suggested, his usefulness and their gratitude. The light from their school-houses spoke of his services to their education. The very sight of their graves brought back to their hearts his tender devotion to their sons. And the papers and the wires with the rising of almost every sun bore to their pure bosoms the news of his success, his triumphs, and his honors. They were proud of him; they admired him—they loved him. These, these were the foundations, the solid foundations, of his place in their minds and in their hearts. From the wind-beaten and storm-bleached capes of Hatteras to the dark blue mountain tops that divide North Carolina and Tennessee there is not a spot from which the name of Vance is not echoed with honor and love. But his influence and his fame were not confined within State lines.

In New England the sons of the brave Puritans admired his love of liberty, his independence of thought, his freedom of speech, his contempt for pretensions, and his abhorrence of deceit. The hardy miners in the far West and on the Pacific hills felt his friendship and were grateful for his services. Virginia loved him as the vindicator of her imperiled rights and honor. From the farms and fields and firesides of the husbandmen of the Republic there came to him the greeting of friends, for he was always the advocate of low taxes and equal rights and privileges to all men. From all the South he was looked upon as the representative of their sorrow and the example of their honor; and all over the civilized world the people of Israel—"the scattered nation"—everywhere bowed with uncovered heads to the brave man who had rendered his noble testimony and a tribute to the virtues of their race. Even the officers, the sentinels, and watchmen over him in the Old Capitol Prison, in which he was confined on the alleged and wrongful charge that he had violated the laws of war, were spellbound by his genial spirit and became his devoted friends up to the hour of his death. His genius, his ability, his humanity, his long-continued public service, his great physical suffering, a martyrdom to his duty, the sorcery of his wit, the magic of his humor, and the courage of his convictions had attracted the universal sympathy and admiration of the American people.

In the brief summary in the Directory is embraced a great life: County attorney, member of the State house of commons; Representative in two Congresses; captain and colonel in the Southern army; three times elected Governor of his State, and four times elected to the Senate of the United States. What a record and what a combination! A great statesman, a good soldier, a rare scholar, a successful lawyer, an orator of surpassing power and eloquence, and a man popular and beloved as few men have ever been!

Great in peace and great in war, equal to every fortune, superior to adversity, and, greater still, superior to prosperity! Successful in everything which he attempted, eminent in every field in which he appeared, and fitted for every effort which he undertook!

He was master of political science and distinguished in scholarship and literature. His political speeches were models of popular oratory and his literary addresses were compositions of chaste excellence. He wrote an electric editorial and drafted a legislative bill with equal clearness and brevity. His pen and his tongue were of equal quality. He used both with equal power. He wrote much; he spoke more. Everything emanating from him wore his own likeness. He borrowed from no man. He imitated no man and no man could imitate him. He was unique, original, wonderful, incomprehensible unless he was a genius with faculties and powers of extraordinary and exceptional character.

His temper was admirable, calm, well balanced, serene. He cared less for trifles than any man I ever knew. He brushed them away as a lion shakes the dust from his mane. In this respect he was a giant. He was like Samson breaking the frail withes that bound his limbs. He was never confused, rarely impatient, seldom nervous, and never weak.

He was merciful in the extreme. Suffering touched him to the quick. He was compassion itself to distress. He was as tender as a gentle woman to the young, the weak, the feeble. He was full of charity to all men, charitable to human frailty in every shape and form and phase. He had deep, powerful impulses, strong and passionate resentments; in the heat of conflict he was inexorable, but his generosity, his magnanimity, his sense of justice were deeper and stronger and better than the few passing passions of his proud nature. To his family and friends he was all tenderness and indulgence. His great heart always beat in duty, with sympathy, with the highest chivalry to woman.

· · ·

On the night of the 16th of April last we took his casket from these walls. We bore it across the Potomac—through the bosom of Virginia, close by the grave of Washington, almost in sight of the tombs of Jefferson and Madison, over the James, over the North and the South Roanoke, over the unknown border line of the sister States—to the sad heart of his mother State. The night was beautiful. The white stars shed their hallowed radiance upon earth and sky. The serenity was lovely. The whole heavens almost seemed a happy reunion of the constellations. With the first light of day the people, singly, in groups, in companies, in crowds, in multitudes, met us everywhere along the way—both sexes—all ages—all races—all classes and conditions. Their sorrow was like the gathering clouds in morning, ready to drop every moment in showers.

We carried him to the State house in Raleigh, the scene of his greatest trials and grandest triumphs; the heart of the State melted over her dead son. Her brightest jewel had been taken away! We left Raleigh in the evening, and passing over the Neuse, over the Yadkin, over the Catawba, up to the summit of the Blue Ridge, we placed the urn with its noble dust on the brow of his own mountain, the mountain he loved so well. There he sleeps in peace and honor. On that exalted spot the willow and the cypress, emblems of sorrow and mourning, can not grow, but the bay and the laurel, the trees of fame, will there flourish and bloom in perpetual beauty and glory. There will his great spirit, like an eternal sentinel of liberty and truth, keep watch over his people.

Senators, I feel how unable I have been to perform this sacred duty. It would have been one of the supreme joys of my life to have done justice to the life and character of this great and good man, to have enshrined his memory in eloquence like his own. But whatever may have been the faults of these words, I have spoken from a heart full of sorrow for his death and throbbing with admiration and pride for his virtues.

United States Congress, 53rd, 3rd Session, *Memorial Addresses on Life and Character of Zebulon B. Vance.* (Washington, 1895)

Address at Unveiling of Statue
at Capitol Square

The statue of Zebulon B. Vance on Capitol Square, Raleigh, was unveiled on August 22, 1900. Richard H. Battle, long-time colleague of Vance, was the principal speaker. Here are excerpts from his address:

Z. B. VANCE.

——————

RICHARD H. BATTLE.*

——————

I will be pardoned for a personal allusion in saying that I was selected to address you on this interesting occasion, rather than an orator like Ransom, Waddell, Jarvis, Bennett, Robbins, or some other eloquent man associated with him in public life, because it was known to those having the selection in charge that I was more intimately acquainted with Vance than any of them, and that I probably best knew the thoughts of his heart and the motives of his conduct. Such I believe to be the fact. We were contemporaries at Chapel Hill, and fellow members of the same literary society, he entering as a law student and taking a partial course with the senior class, when a young man just twenty-one, and I an impressionable youth of fifteen years. I was his private secretary from the day of his inauguration as Governor, September 8, 1862, for two years, and then, by his appointment, State Auditor, and often his legal counsel in questions and cases growing out of the

* From an address delivered at the unveiling of the Vance statue in Capitol Square, Raleigh, N. C., August 22, 1900.

conscript law, until we left the Capitol, April 12, 1865, the day before its occupation by Sherman. During these three years, while his labors were herculean and his anxieties intense, I was in daily association with him, sometimes in the privacy of his home, and I had the best of opportunities to hear what he said, to see what he did, and to sound the depths of his great soul. Then and ever afterwards he treated me with the kindness and confidence and (may I not say?) with the affection of an older brother. I would have been blind indeed not to have learned his real character, and callous indeed not to have felt for him the affection of a brother.

If then, in a cursory review of the leading events of his life and an attempt to delineate his character, I seem to be influenced by a natural bias, I can only say, I try to tell things as they were, and remind you that I am only giving reasons for the verdict of the people, attested by what we see here to-day, that taking into consideration the many elements which constitute greatness, and measuring all her sons by its many standards, in all the history of North Carolina Zebulon B. Vance was her greatest son. For Senatorial wisdom and the exercise of the civic virtues of a Cincinnatus, we may assign the pre-eminence to Nathaniel Macon; for polished statesmanship, in times of peace, to William Gaston or William A. Graham; for profundity as an advocate and a logician, to George E. Badger; as a great jurist, to Thomas Ruffin; for the graces of magnificent oratory, to Willie P. Mangum; for the talent to develop the internal resources of a State, to John M. Morehead; but in achievement as a leader, in inducing others to follow him by the strength of his personality, for what he said and what he did, in peace and in war, towards shaping the destiny of the State and for promoting the welfare of the people, Vance was ahead of them all.

Some writer has said that it takes three generations to

make a gentleman. The history of Western North Carolina shows that it took three generations of heroic and
patriotic citizens to make our Vance. His father was David
Vance, and his mother, Margaret, a daughter of Zebulon
Baird; and the Vances and the Bairds, sturdy Scotch-Irish
people, from Kings Mountain down, were patriots and
leading citizens. He inherited from such ancestors a spirit
of independence, a love of freedom, and a reverence for the
true, the pure, and the good, along with a strong mind and
sound body. He inherited little else; for his father died when
he was a boy, leaving a widow and eight children to be supported on a small farm, and besides a few slaves, scarcely
more personal property than was necessary to pay his debts
and funeral expenses. So Zebulon was a poor boy, who had
to make his own way in the world. When about twelve
years old, his father sent him across the mountains on
horse-back, to enter as a pupil in a high school, known as
Washington College, in East Tennessee; but he was soon
called home by the mortal illness of his father, whose bed-
side he reached only in time to see him die. All the education, in schools, he then had or acquired afterwards, until
he became of age, was obtained in little schools in the neigh-
borhood of his native home. That home was about ten miles
northwest of Asheville, in the county of Buncombe, and
but a few hundred yards from the French Broad River.
Born and reared in the shadows of the highest peaks of the
Blue Ridge Mountains, with Mount Mitchell and Pisgah
in full view from the surrounding hills, and with the music
of the mountain streams and birds in the air, the boy, endowed with uncommon intelligence and an active imagination, was early inspired with a love of his native land, while
his soul was attuned to the poetry of nature. Patriotism and
poetry, lofty sentiments, are closely akin; and these sentiments most abound where nature is most picturesque and
grand; where the mists of morning are dispelled from glow-

ing peaks by the rising sun, and the lengthening shadows
of evening change the form and color of cloud, forest, and
mountain; where rushing streams and leaping cascades
furnish to eyes which can see, and ears attuned to hear, a
beauty and charm unknown to dwellers among the foot-
hills or on the level lands below. The intelligent inhabitants
of such a region learn to love their homes intensely, and are
ever ready to fight and die for them. So it was, ever, with
the Swiss and the Highland Scotch, where mountains
echoed and re-echoed their patriotic songs; and we read in
sacred history that when the chosen people were taken by
their conquerors from the mountains and hills of Galilee
and Judea, and carried captive to the plains of Babylon,
they "hung their harps upon the willows" and wept tears
of despair for their country. Certain it is that, in my obser-
vation of the great and patriotic men of our State, her two
most devoted sons were born and reared among the mountains of Buncombe: David L. Swain and Zebulon B. Vance.
Inspired alike by the poetry of the Bible and of nature,
their souls were open to all high and patriotic emotions. At
first their love was given to their native homes; but as the
sphere of their lives and labor widened it was extended to
State and country. Was it due to this special quality or virtue, apparent in them, that they, each, became the Chief
Magistrate of the State at the early age of thirty-two years,
when younger than any other in our long list of Governors?

· · ·

But Vance's right to the epithet of "The War Governor
of the South" is due as much to the earnest support of the
Confederate cause by his State through him as its executive
head, as to what he did for its people, their protection under
the law, and their general welfare. For nearly three years,
from September 8, 1862, to the evening he left Raleigh,
April 12, 1865, to avoid capture by Sherman, he did all

that vigilance, zeal, and energy could do to have and keep every man to whom Lee, Johnston, and others were entitled, as soldiers, at the front. To him it is due, largely, that the seventy-five regiments and some unattached commands from North Carolina were kept fuller than those from any other State, notwithstanding that the bodies of more North Carolina dead strewed the battlefields of the country than those of any other State; that quite one-sixth of the Confederate troops hailed from this State; that we had a soldier for nearly every voter; and that one-fifth the Confederates surrendered by Lee at Appomattox, and one-half surrendered by Johnston at Greensboro, were North Carolinians. And what was the testimony of our great captain, Robert E. Lee, as to the value of Vance's service to his army? In the winter of 1863–'64, in view of the disasters of Gettysburg and Vicksburg the summer before, desertion was depleting his ranks and despondency was settling like a pall over his army and the country. Governor Vance saw that the good name of his State and its soldiers was imperiled, and he was moved to leave his office at Raleigh, visit the army, and make to brigades and divisions, in which there were North Carolina troops, those wonderful speeches whereby hope was substituted for despondency, and our battered regiments, from other States as well as this, were nerved again with the courage and resolve to do or to die. Was it not partly due to this campaign of oratory that General Lee, who had double or treble his numbers and the world's resources at his command, from the Rapidan to Petersburg, and to make himself the peer of Hannibal, Frederick, and Washington, and his noble army to share the immortality of the Spartan band at Thermopylæ? It is reported that he said that Vance's visits and speeches were worth as much to him as 50,000 recruits. After hearing some of those speeches, Gen. J. E. B. Stuart, who followed him from corps to corps and from division to division, asserted that if oratory is to be measured by its effects, Governor Vance was the greatest orator that ever lived.

· · ·

Resolving to begin the practice of law again, he settled in Charlotte. He first practiced in partnership with Col. H. C. Jones and Gen. Robert D. Johnston, and afterwards as a partner of Maj. Clement Dowd. His circuit was extensive, and his practice brought him fair remuneration, but it did not occupy all of his time, and his evenings at home and on circuit, when not in conference with client or associate counsel, were employed in the preparation of lectures, by the delivery of which he could add to his income for the support of his family and to pay debts incurred before the courts were fairly opened. Some of these lectures were eloquent, and exhibited much literary skill, and they were all interesting and instructive. One, on "The Scattered Nation," suggested, doubtless, by the high qualities he observed in some of his Jewish friends and neighbors in Statesville and Charlotte, gave him real fame as a lecturer, and was delivered with great acceptability to Jew and Gentile, by request, in different parts of the country, North and South. One, on the "Demagogue," in the derivative sense of the word, as a *leader of the people*, should be in print. It contains a very amusing account of the experiences of an enterprising canvasser for Congress, doubtless his own, and some excellent lessons to public speakers as to the use of illustrations and anecdotes in popular speeches. His anecdotes were so amusing that they were, after every speech, widely circulated; and not to repeat well-known stories he must either have had a wonderfully large repertory or have manufactured many of them for the occasion.

Governor Vance was accustomed, on account of having devoted so much of his time to other things than the law, to speak lightly, with his friends, of his accomplishments as a lawyer; but he was well-grounded in legal principles, and his sense of justice was so strong, and he was so quick to apprehend a point suggested by Judge or counsel, that his client's cause seldom suffered from his want of technical knowledge; and his influence with the juries was more than sufficient to make up for any deficiency in that direction. An opponent in some of his cases, himself an able and successful lawyer, said, after some of Vance's triumphs, that a law ought to be passed by the Legislature denying the *last speech* to Vance before a Mecklenburg jury. His quickness and knowledge of human nature made him very skilful in examination of witnesses, while by unexpected repartee, by apt illustration and mirthful stories, he often upset the decorum of the Court and convulsed jurors and bystanders.

·   ·   ·

Elected to the Senate about the last of November, 1878, and January, 1885, and January, 1891, he served his State and country in that great field of labor from the day he was sworn in in March, 1879, until stricken down by disease, a short time before his death in April, 1894. How he served, how he labored, how he bore himself in the hard-fought battles of those fifteen years, against open enemy or insidious foe; how vigilant he was to protect the liberties of the people and defend the fair name of his own constituents and their brethren of the South; how by incessant toil, day and night, which caused him the loss of an eye and then shortened his days, he mastered the great questions of the tariff and finance and became the recognized leader of his party on those questions; how he used the battle-axe of logic or the scimitar of irony and wit, with equal ease, as exigency demanded; how by courage, candor, and sincerity, in all he said and did, on the floor and in committee-rooms, he commanded the respect and confidence of all honest adversaries, and undoubting support of his followers; how by kindly, if bluff, courtesy and merry jest, in lobby and cloakroom, he overcame the prejudice of Northern Senators, and made personal friends of political opponents, how he enlivened the dullest debates by unexpected sallies, neat epigrams, and witty illustrations; how his arguments were so interesting that the seats were better filled when he spoke than when others had the floor, and how crowded galleries hung upon his words; how his weight and influence in the councils of his party, in the House as well as the Senate, were ever growing; how his solemn words as he spoke for the last time, September 1, 1893, from his place in the Senate Chamber, warning the people of the country against the encroachments of the money power and its allies, sounded through the land like the tones of a fire-bell at night, are all part of the history of the times.

The eulogies of him, as orator, statesman, and man, pronounced ten months after his death, and in words well weighed, by leading men of both parties, are sufficient to satisfy his most ardent friends, and justify me fully in saying that in the opinion of his fellows he stood in the forefront of the great men of the country, and that in him passed away the most interesting personality of our day.

· · ·

It is said "that the greatness of most men diminishes with the distance." That it was not so with Vance, among his intimate friends and in his own home, I think I have shown. That it was not so among his neighbors in Charlotte, where he so long lived, and that they could not have been party or privy to the little estrangement alluded to, conclusively appears from an account given by the *Charlotte Observer* of his last public appearance in that city. It was on the evening of November 1, 1892, and the *occasion* was that Mr. Ham, a distinguished Georgia orator and wit, by invitation, addressed the citizens in the largest auditorium of the city. At the conclusion of his speech, "Vance! Vance!" was the sound which burst continuously from the immense audience, as the applause for Mr. Ham subsided, and as the noble, loved "Zeb" arose, the people went wild; old men, young men, women and children, jumped to their feet, waving handkerchiefs and hats, and cheering until the very building seemed to rock. Not a person in the house remained seated. Many stood on the benches; hats were thrown up, and such an expression of love, affection, and esteem was never shown to any son of North Carolina at any time or anywhere, as was expressed in the great ovation over Vance. On the rostrum every man rose, and following Mr. Ham's lead, all waved their handkerchiefs and cheered for fully ten minutes. It was a great demonstration, and one that did honor even to the loved Senator. As he stood on the rostrum, amid the deafening cheers of his people, he looked like a grand chieftan leading his people, and guiding them simply by his presence. It was a scene the like of which was never seen in Charlotte before.

·   ·   ·

Born May 13, 1830, and dying April 14, 1894, how much of labor well done, of duty well performed, of glory nobly achieved, in those sixty-four years of mortal life! In the admiration and gratitude of his State he will continue to live as long as North Carolina shall be a State! And in that other life, the higher life, he will live, we fondly trust, to all eternity, in that home prepared by Him who says to every son of man who has done his duty here: "Well done, thou good and faithful servant; enter thou into the joy of thy Lord."

Literary and Historical Activities in North Carolina, 1900–1905 (Raleigh, 1907).

Unveiling of Statue at Statuary Hall

The statue of Zebulon B. Vance was unveiled in Statuary Hall in the Capitol in Washington in 1916. Four addresses were delivered in Statuary Hall, three in the Senate, and nine in the House of Representatives. Here are excerpts from the address of Locke Craig, Governor of North Carolina:

ADDRESS OF HON. LOCKE CRAIG

And now, Mr. President [turning to the Vice President], the State of North Carolina presents through you to the United States the statue of ZEBULON BAIRD VANCE. This is done by authority of a resolution of the General Assembly of North Carolina passed without dissent. The recognition of VANCE as the greatest of our men, and the placing of his statue in this pantheon of the Nation, is but the execution of the judgment of all of the people of North Carolina. His personality, his character, and his deeds confer upon him the right to stand here, a peer among the foremost of the Republic.

Our State has not been in a hurry to occupy the two places assigned to her in this hall. In preferring VANCE as the first, she has been mindful of her obligation to consider with justice all of her noble sons. And she has realized, too, her obligation to do justice to herself. This statue shall be a perpetual memorial of him and of her. The State must be judged by the best that she can produce. He is our most precious gift to the world. Since we have set him up as the finest conception and expression of North Carolina life, he must be the standard by which this and coming generations shall measure the significance and worth of the State.

He was a son of North Carolina, bone of her bone, and flesh of her flesh. He was born and reared among the mountains, and was of Scotch-Irish lineage, but his sympathies were not limited by sectional lines nor by the dogmas of creeds. Wherever he went, among all classes and conditions of men, from the humblest to the greatest, he was *primus inter pares*, and exemplified the universal brotherhood. In fashionable salons, among scholars and statesmen, he was simple, natural, brilliant, easily the center. With the same unpretentious manner, on terms of perfect equality he charmed the men in working clothes, with rough hands, and was loved by them as their wiser and stronger brother, whose fidelity could never be doubted. He taught dignity to nobility. He was "a legist among the lawyers, a sidereal among the astronomers."

VANCE was trusted and honored and loved by the people of North Carolina as no other man has been. He was elected and reelected to the places of highest honor. He was vested with the greatest trust and called in every crisis to do the foremost part. From the time that he was 30 years old until the day of his death at the age of 64 he was the unrivaled leader. Faith in his loyalty and prowess never faltered.

Preeminent merit is not always the necessary prerequisite to high official position, but for 30 years, in times of war and revolution, disaster and suffering, VANCE was the chosen champion of the people. He declared their policies. He voiced their highest aspirations. He was always in the fiercest of the conflict to meet and to overcome with blow for blow the mightiest that opposed. He was the voice of the State, the incarnation of her passion, her hopes, her determination, and her purpose. He was the leader to call her to duty, to rescue her victoriously from ruin and strife into the way of peace and to point her to a triumphant destiny. This entitles him to a place among the immortals.

· · ·

In 1879 VANCE took his seat in the Senate of the United States. The volcanic force and fire of the period of storm and revolution subsided into the calm and clear strength and dignity of the Senator. At no period in our history have there been so many men in the Senate of power and accomplished statesmanship. Every State sent her strongest men. The floor of the Senate was the arena of intellectual giants. There were Blaine, of Maine; Edmunds and Morrill, of Vermont; Hoar, of Massachusetts; Conkling, of New York; Bayard, of Delaware; Ransom, of North Carolina; Hampton, of South Carolina; Benjamin Hill, of Georgia; Morgan, of Alabama; Lamar, of Mississippi; Blackburn, of Kentucky; Vest, of Missouri; Voorhees, of Indiana; Thurman, of Ohio; Ingalls, of Kansas. In this great company VANCE was recognized as the equal of any, an intellectual gladiator who never lowered his arm, a statesman who dedicated himself to labor and to the service of the State and of the whole Nation. He mastered the problems of his time, and added to his national fame. His speeches gave evidence, not only of his known ability, but of classic culture. In debates on the policies and fundamental questions of controlling importance he was generally put forward as the spokesman of his party. He was by constitution and by culture a democrat. He was the unrelenting foe of unjust privilege of all kinds, the apostle of equal rights. He delivered the faith that is now the creed of Democracy. For half a century the advocates of political dogmas have conjured with his name, or tried to conjure with it.

There was nothing of the demagogue about VANCE. He was nearly always on the popular side, but often by his own genius he made his side popular. He was one of those men of genius of universal type. He was one of the people, in full accord and sympathy with them. His single purpose was the common good, with a passion for justice and against unfairness and oppression. Gen. Theodore F. Davidson, a kinsman of VANCE, who knew him perhaps more intimately than any living man, says of him:

Another characteristic particularly in public matters, was his capacity to divine the right; it seemed to me that with less effort than any public man of whom I have any knowledge, he could almost instantly comprehend a public question with its results, by intuition. This quality was an endowment of nature, developed and strengthened by the circumstances of his unusual career.

Another distinguishing characteristic which made him the first of the "leaders of men," was his absolute devotion to that which he believed to be the best for his country and his people. I do not believe there ever was a moment in his life when he was not perfectly willing to offer himself and all he had for the benefit of his countrymen without the slightest consideration whether it brought to him compensation in any form.

If you strike the chord of a musical instrument in the midst of other musical instruments, all of the chords that are in perfect harmony will vibrate with the same rhythm. VANCE was in harmony with the people. The same causes that stirred them stirred him. He uttered the dominant note. His vision was farther and clearer. His conception stronger. He expressed what they vaguely felt, and what they had been longing to hear, and he gave tone and unity to their thought, their aspirations, and their life.

· · ·

VANCE never quailed nor bowed the knee to power. When he was down, when his enemies were in control and his future seemed darkest he wrote the following letter:

To the Editor of the New York World:

I see by the public prints that Gen. Kilpatrick has decorated me with his disapprobation before the people of Pennsylvania. He informs them, substantially, that he tamed me by capturing me and riding me 200 miles on a bareback mule. I will do him the justice to say that he knew that was a lie when he uttered it.

I surrendered to Gen. Schofield at Greensboro, N. C., on the 2d day of May, 1865, who told me to go to my home and remain there, saying that if he got any orders to arrest me he would send there for me. Accordingly I went home, and there remained until I was arrested on the 13th of May by a detachment of 300 Cavalry, under Maj. Porter, of Harrisburg, from whom I received nothing but kindness and courtesy. I came in a buggy to Salisbury, where we took the cars.

I saw no mule on the trip, yet I thought I saw an ass at the general's headquarters; this impression has since been confirmed.

Respectfully, yours,

Z. B. VANCE.

His humor was inimitable; it was spontaneous. Audiences were convulsed with laughter by his witticisms and his stories; but his humor was always an incident. It always illustrated. It was always used for a purpose. It was overwhelming and brought his antagonist irresistibly into ridicule. When the southern leaders in Congress were accused of disloyalty, he said:

> What motive have we to injure this country? Having surrendered the doctrine of secession and abandoned any intention whatsoever to divide this Union, how could we expect that the democracy to which we belong could obtain and hold the control of the Government except by showing the people by our acts that we are patriotically desirous of promoting its welfare and its glory. But you say you distrust these expressions. My friends, in your hearts you do not. On the contrary, a man who has offered his blood once for his plighted faith you believe when he plights his faith again. There is not a southern rebel, no matter how bitter and rampant he may have been, that you have not received with arms widespread and rewarded with offices of honor and trust who came to you with craven repentance on his tongue, ready to vote the Republican ticket and eating dirt with the same gluttonous appetite with which he once ate fire. You profess to believe him, but you despise him in your hearts. You are not alarmed to receive him and you cast no suspicion upon his professions of sincerity, though, as has more than once happened, he asks you to believe he tells the truth to-day because he told a lie yesterday.

His personal appearance was unique. He did not look like other men. No man who saw him ever forgot him. His magnetism charmed with a peculiar and indescribable power. When you looked upon him, you knew that you beheld the lion-hearted leader of men.

When known and understood, men of all parties admired and honored him for his convictions, his courage, his kindness of heart, his abiding loyalty and devotion to the whole country.

When he died the State was awed into a solemnity that we had not known. It was realized that the foremost had fallen. The train bearing him for the last time to the bosom of the mountains that bore him and nurtured him passed through the State while the assembled people with uncovered heads bowed and wept. Meetings were held in almost every county in expression of universal sorrow. The State was his funeral cortege.

No hollow formalist was he, deceptive and self-deceptive, ghastly to the natural sense, but a very man, fiery, real, from the great fire bosom of nature herself.

United States Congress, 64th, 1st Session, *Proceedings in Statuary Hall, U.S. Senate and House of Representatives Upon Unveiling of Statue of Zebulon B. Vance* (Washington, 1917).

THE SCULPTOR

GUTZON BORGLUM

Born in Idaho, March 25, 1867; son of Dr. James de la Mothe Borglum and Ida (Michelson) Borglum. Educated in the public schools of Fremont and Omaha, Nebr., and at St. Mary's College, Kans. Studied art in San Francisco, and went to Paris in 1890, working and studying in Académie Julien and Ecole des Beaux Arts. Exhibited as painter and sculptor in Paris Salon, in Spain in 1892, and in California in 1893–94; returned East and went to London in 1896, remaining there and in Paris until 1901. Has been in New York City since 1902. Exhibited in Paris in 1896 and 1901; held successful "one-man" exhibit in London; received gold medal for sculpture at Louisiana Purchase Exposition. Was sculptor for work on Cathedral of St. John the Divine, New York; Sheridan Equestrian Monument in Washington, D. C.; colossal marble head of Lincoln and the statue of Zebulon Baird Vance in the Capitol Building; figure of America on American Republics Building; Mares of Diomedes (bronze), Metropolitan Museum, New York; The Atlas (marble), New York, etc. Member Royal Society of British Artists, Société National des Beaux Arts, and Architectural League. Clubs: Metropolitan (Washington, D. C.), Players, Camp Fire, Lotos, Fencers, City, and Balsam Lake Club, New York.

Address at Dedication of Monument
at Asheville

The monument in memory of Zebulon B. Vance on Pack Square in Asheville, North Carolina, was dedicated on May 10, 1898. An address was delivered by R. L. Taylor, Governor of Tennessee. Here are excerpts from his address:

ADDRESS OF HON. R. L. TAYLOR

... Never again will his people be entranced by his eloquence, nor the enraptured multitudes listen to the music of his voice. Never again will solemn Senators turn away from their dignity to delight in the glow of his genial spirit. The warmth of joy has departed from his lips; the star that once shed glory upon the old North state has set forever. A coffin, a winding-sheet, six feet by two of Mother Earth, a monument, and precious memories are all that is left of the orator and actor, the humanitarian, the statesman and patriot. . . . It would be presumptuous folly in me to parade in your presence to-day the noble traits of his character and the thrilling events of his life, which have enriched the history of his state and made his name immortal. They are thoroughly known to you all.

When I was a barefooted boy romping among the hills of Tennessee the news of his fame and the tidings of his marvelous campaigns used to come floating over the mountains. The boys heard his yarns, and rolled on the floor with merriment; the old ladies sat at the fireside and cackled at his anecdotes, and the sturdy old farmers listened to his stories in the fields, and stopped their plows to laugh.

· · ·

No power ever checked the triumphal march of the youthful mountaineer to the glorious destiny which awaited him.

No political foe ever withstood his wit and humor and logic and his matchless eloquence. They were his passports to the Legislature and to Congress while yet a youth in his twenties, and as he grew older his powers developed. His popularity was unparalleled, his influence was invincible. Through all his long and brilliant career his love for humanity never waned and his devotion to his country never cooled—always ready with a charming story to tell, always quick at repartee. And yet his logic was as convincing as the sword of Stonewall Jackson at Manassas or as the guns of Dewey at Manila. He was as honest as Davis, humorous as Lincoln, eloquent as Daniels, as true to the hopes that perished at Appomattox as Gordon and Forrest, and afterward as loyal to the Union as Wheeler and Lee, who now wear the blue.

Senator Vance was a splendid thinker and a statesman of rare ability, but he always looked on the bright side of things, and no music was half so sweet to him as the songs and laughter of the merry throngs of country folks who gathered about him on every occasion with shouts and hallelujahs to while away the happy hours. And thus his busy life was spent in adding to the sum of human happiness. . . . I would rather trust my life and liberty in the hands of a laughing fool than in the hands of a frowning tyrant. Nations do not suffer when their rulers sincerely smile and govern with love and mercy; but God pity the land whose ruler frowns and rules with an iron rod, and God pity the ruler himself, for the harvest of his frowns is death! . . .

The life of Washington eclipses the glory of Cæsar, and the beautiful reign of Victoria outshines the romantic record of Napoleon's rise and fall. . . .

Laughter and love and hope and happiness are the companions of pleasure, the patrons and allies of civilization, the handmaids of religion, the evangels of God.

Senator Vance lived and loved and laughed and labored

for his people and for humanity. He planted the flowers of mirth and joy in the hearts of others, and labored on until the winter of age whitened his head with the snow that never melts. But there was no snow upon his heart: it was always summer there.

Confederate Veteran, Vol. 6, No. 5, Nashville, Tenn., May, 1898, p. 198.

Selected Bibliography

Barrett, John G. *The Civil War in North Carolina.* (Chapel Hill, N. C., 1963).

Camp, Cordelia. *Governor Vance: A Life For Young People.* (Asheville, N. C., 1961).

Cannon, Elizabeth R., editor. *My Beloved Zebulon.* (Chapel Hill, N. C., 1971).

Claiborne, Jack, and Price, William, editors. *Discovering North Carolina.* (Chapel Hill, N. C., 1991).

Coates, Albert. *Three North Carolinians Who Have Stood Up To Be Counted for the Bill of Rights.* (Chapel Hill, N. C., 1973).

Cooper, Richard. *Zeb Vance: Leader in War and Peace.* (Raleigh, N. C., 1985).

Dowd, Clement. *Life of Zebulon B. Vance.* (Charlotte, N. C., 1897).

Johnston, Frontis W., editor. *The Papers of Zebulon B. Vance.* (Raleigh, N. C., 1963).

Kratt, Mary Norton. *Charlotte — Spirit of the New South.* (Winston-Salem, N. C., 1992).

Lefler, Hugh T., and Newsome, Albert R. *North Carolina: The History of a Southern State.* (Chapel Hill, N. C., 1954).

North Carolina Historical Commission. *Literary and Historical Activities.* 1900–1905. Contains the address of Richard H. Battle delivered at unveiling of Vance statue in Capitol Square, Raleigh, N. C., in 1900.

Phillips, Russell. *Hooray for Vance!* American Mercury XXII, 1931.

Reed, Thomas B., editor. *Modern Eloquence.* (Philadelphia, Pa., 1900).

Sandburg, Carl. *Abraham Lincoln: The War Years.* 4 Volumes. (New York, 1939).

Shirley, Frank Ray. *Zebulon Vance, Tarheel Spokesman.* (Charlotte, N. C., 1962).

Shurter, Edwin DuBois, editor. *Oratory of the South.* (New York, 1908).

Speizman, Morris. *The Jews of Charlotte.* (Charlotte, N. C., 1978).

Szittya, Ruth O. *Man to Match the Mountains: The Childhood of Zebulon B. Vance.* (Asheville, N. C., 1980).

Tucker, Glenn. *Zeb Vance: Champion of Personal Freedom.* (Indianapolis, Ind., 1965).

United States Congress, 53rd, 3rd Session, *Memorial Addresses on Life and Character of Zebulon B. Vance.* (Washington, D. C., 1895).

United States Congress, 64th, 1st Session. *Proceedings in Statuary Hall,*

U.S. Senate and House of Representatives upon unveiling of Statue of Zebulon B. Vance. (Washington, D. C., 1917).

Vance, Zebulon B. *The Scattered Nation.* (New York, 1904).

Vance, Zebulon B. *The Scattered Nation.* (New York, 1916).

Vance, Zebulon B. *The Scattered Nation.* (Raleigh, N. C., 1928).

Walser, Richard. *Tar Heel Laughter.* (Chapel Hill, N. C., 1974).

Womble, Iris W. *Zeb Vance: Tarheel Tribune.* (Florida, 1949).

Yates, Richard E. *The Confederacy and Zeb Vance.* (Tuscaloosa, Ala., 1958).

Index

PERMISSIONS

Grateful acknowledgment is made for permission to quote from the following works:

Abraham Lincoln: The War Years (1939) by Carl Sandburg, by permission from Harcourt, Brace Co.

The Civil War in North Carolina (1963) by John D. Barrett, by permission from University of North Carolina Press.

The Friars and the Jews (1982) by Jeremy Cohen, by permission from Cornell University Press.

Has God Rejected His People? (1982) by Clark M. Williamson, published by Abingdon Press. Permission granted by Clark M. Williamson.

Zebulon Vance, Tarheel Spokesman (1962) by Franklin Ray Shirley, by permission of Heritage Printers, Inc., successor to McNally & Loftin.